THE CHALLENGE OF FATHERHOOD

Thoughts on the Priesthood

Massimo Camisasca
The Challenge of Fatherhood
Thoughts on the Priesthood

Translated by Adrian Walker
Edited by Jonah Lynch

FRATERNITY
OF ST. CHARLES
Passion for the glory of Christ

Book design by Melissa Galliani

Title of the original Italian publication:
La sfida della paternità
© Edizioni San Paolo 2003
Used with permission.

ISBN: 978-0-9823561-3-5

Priestly Fraternity of the Missionaries of St. Charles Borromeo, Inc.
www.fraternityofsaintcharles.org

Massimo Camisasca

THE CHALLENGE OF FATHERHOOD

Thoughts on the Priesthood

Contents

Preface

This book gathers together some of the talks that I have given to the seminarians and priests of the Priestly Fraternity of the Missionaries of St. Charles Borromeo, a community born from the charism of Communion and Liberation in 1985. The Fraternity numbers today some 100 definitive members and 40 seminarians. I have guided them as superior from the beginning, and so have had many opportunities to speak to my brothers, young and old. And all towards one end: their education and mine.

I would now like to offer anyone who might be interested a small selection of these talks of mine, which I have collected around the theme of priestly life.

In particular, the first chapter brings together some thoughts on the ordained priesthood and its place in the Church and in the life of man. The second part, comprising chapters two, three, and four, sets forth the main lines of education in the basic dimensions of Christian life (obedience, poverty, virginity), which in my day were things that fascinated me in the teaching of Don Giussani. The third and concluding part, containing chapters five and six, is dedicated to paternity and sexuality.

I hope to offer material for meditation to those who, in making use of it, will become my companions in our journey towards the Father.

I
Priesthood

Vocation

God gives every man only one vocation, and every man is
called to discover the one purpose and direction of his life.
Vocations are not added one on top of another; in the
course of his life, a person does not get called now to this,
now to that: there is one and only one vocation for each
person. God did not conceive of me first as a living being,
then as a Christian, then as a priest. If, at a certain point in
my life, I perceived that the priestly vocation was the true
one for me, it was because I recognized that it was not just
one option among others for me to choose, but that it was
how Christ wanted me to follow him. God did not conceive
of my mother first as a person who was to receive the gift
of life, then as a Christian, then as a woman destined to
meet my father. When God conceives of our face, he conceives of it in its complete form, even though each of us
has to achieve it in time as a progressive discovery. And
each one of us experiences his own freedom as the possibility of corresponding to the Father's will, to God's will.

This progressive discovery of our personal destiny usually happens through difficulty and pain. It is often through
suffering that we begin truly to know. We come to understand as if by putting together the pieces of a puzzle or
weaving together the strands of a tapestry. In God, however,
there is no progression. He has a perfectly clear idea of what

our face looks like, and he is patient enough to let it be unveiled before our eyes, too: slowly, sometimes even through contradictions, zig-zags, second thoughts. This is why we must not make the mistake of thinking, say, that something that blocks our path for a moment thwarts it radically. It is just a moment of darkness that we need in order to fall in love again with the light, to rediscover the light, to walk more resolutely in and towards it. Our freedom matures along the path of this "groping" (see Acts 17:27).

Our existence is the progressive unveiling of the benevolent plan that God has for our lives. Knowing this makes our existence truly exciting, centering it on the one and only truth that endures, explains, and enables us to get through difficulties, to understand trials, and, above all, to accept them.

Now, there is an event in which the total, definitive word about our lives has been spoken. This event is called Baptism.

We cannot understand the priestly vocation, or any other vocation, for that matter, unless we think of it as a way in which Christ calls us to live out our Baptism. The Sacrament of Orders and the Sacrament of Marriage are rooted in, and make sense only as flowerings of, Baptism. For Baptism gives birth to the new man, and that is what everything in the Church is about.

Saint Paul often repeated this feelingly and without ifs, ands, or buts. After having spoken of our liberation from the law, for example, the Apostle writes: "Do you not know that all of us who have been baptized into Christ Jesus were baptized into his death? We were therefore buried with him by Baptism into death, so that as Christ was raised from the dead by the glory of the Father, we too might walk in newness of life. For if we have been completely united with him in a death like his, we shall certainly be united with him in a resurrection like his" (Rom 6:3-5). In the act of Baptism, we have been buried, united to Christ in death, in the sense that Baptism has "assimilated" us to his death. The whole of life is the unfolding of this assimilation, and there are times when we experience its hardness and are tempted to reject it. But this is the expereince that we began in Baptism, so that, if we have been united to him in his death, we might be united to him in his Resurrection, as well.

But what, precisely, is this experience of death? And why is it an experience—first ontologically, and only then psychologically—of death in us? It is the experience of the death of the "old man": in Baptism, the old man in us dies, the man who lives in the triple prison of sin, death, and the law (see Rom 6: 6-7). In Baptism, which is Christ's death, the old man, and in him this triple slavery, is crucified. But the Christ who died was also raised from the dead: "as Christ was raised from the dead by the glory of the Father, we too might walk in newness of life" (Rom 6:4). We will live with him and never die again: "Christ being raised from the dead will never die again; death no longer has dominion over him" (Rom 6:9). We thus come to the "new man" Saint Paul speaks of (see Eph 2:14-15; 4:20-24): the free man, the liberated man. And that is what the Christian vocation is: a call to freedom: "for you were called to freedom" (Gal 5:13). Even if the experience of death is still in us, it is no longer a nightmare that darkens our existence, because death is no longer the last word. Our existence is no longer determined by the slavery of sin, because we are forgiven, and by the slavery of the law, because we have been set free from its yoke.

This, then, is the Christian vocation. It displays itself in time as a belonging to Christ: "for as many of you as were baptized into Christ have put on Christ" (Gal 3:27). But what is born in place of the old man? What is this new identity of ours that replaces the identity of the man enslaved to death, sin, and the law? It is Christ himself, however surprising this answer may sound. Christ enters into our life and patterns it on his. Saint Paul says as much in the passage I cited from just now: "for as many of you as were baptized into Christ have put on Christ. There is neither Jew nor Greek [ethnic identity], there is neither slave nor free [social identity], there is neither male nor female [sexual identity]; for you are all one in Christ Jesus" (Gal 3:27-28). This one sentence says two things: your identity no longer gets its ultimate definition from social, ethnic, and sexual criteria, but from the person of Christ who has assimilated you to himself; therefore, you are all assimilated to Christ, you are all one single person.

How Paul concludes this passage is extremely interesting: "and if you are Christ's, then you are Abraham's offspring, heirs according to the promise" (Gal 3:29). This means that Baptism gives birth at once to a new man and to a new people. Paul emphasizes this in another passage: "for by one Spirit we were all baptized into one body" (1 Cor 12:13). Paul always sees the personal and the social dimensions of the new birth together in his letters. Christian vocation is the discovery of one's own identity and of one's own membership in the new people.

In John's Gospel, Jesus himself describes the phenomenon in his conversation with Nicodemus (Jn 3:1-21). Anyone who has been to certain parts of the world like Siberia (as I have) will have a better grasp of Jesus' simile, which is inspired by the experience of a natural environment where the wind blows without any obstacles and so is free suddenly to create new situations. In such places, the wind really does play the role of a generative power. You don't know where it comes from or where it is going, but you observe—and do you ever!—its effects. Something analogous happens in Baptism: you don't know where it's coming from, because it is a birth from above, that is, it brings another kind of origin right into natural life. The new man still has the full natural personality he has by his birth from his mother and father: his intelligence, his affectivity, his passion, his capacity for work, together with his weaknesses. And yet, all of this is informed by another life-principle. It is not simply that one's personal energies get directed to a different goal. No, one receives a new root, which sends its sap coursing through every aspect of one's person.

The Christian vocation takes it shape from the new birth brought about by Baptism. The new man is called to follow Christ and in this way to discover his own identity. What he discovers is not something generic, but the "color" of his own particular way of belonging to the person of Christ and the new people to which he gives birth.

If a man is called to the priestly ministry, then, this ministry is the path along which his Baptism, his lay calling, his Christian vocation are to mature[1]. Nevertheless, the ordained priesthood will gradually reveal to him its very definite particularity, as well. In a letter dated 26 December, 1896, Thérèse of Lisieux wrote the following words to a seminarian: "your part is truly beautiful, because it is the part that Jesus chose for himself"[2]. And that is what the ordained priesthood brings about: a particular identification with Christ's mission.

---

[1] This does not mean, of course, that there is no difference between the priesthood of the baptized and the ordained priesthood. On the contrary, the Church has always affirmed – and even Vatican II underscored this – that there is difference not only of degree, but also of kind, between them. See, for example, *Lumen Gentium*, 10.

[2] Thérèse of Lisieux, "Letter 184," in *Gli Scritti* (Rome: OCD, 1998), 705-708.

The Servant

If I had to think of one expression that could sum up my experience as a priest—with all of the limits that any synthesis is more or less bound to have—I would have to go back to the word "servant." I've returned to this word only after working through a strong, long-standing antipathy to it that was mostly due to how terms like "servant" or "service" became sociological slogans in the Church in the '60's and '70's. Having discovered that they have a different and profound meaning, I realize that they actually shed light on the very essence of the priesthood.

"Servant" and "service" express a "relativity" to the master on whom one depends and to whom one belongs, as well as a "relativity" to a task to be performed. Jesus himself explained the word "servant"—which he used to describe, among other things, the nature of our relationship to him—by saying that the servant does not know his master's secrets, but only what the master asks him to do, adding that he would no longer call us servants, but friends, inasmuch as he would introduce us into the knowledge of every secret (see Jn 15:15). Far from contradicting the use of the word "servant," Jesus' promise, "I no longer call you servants, but friends," actually reinforces it. Indeed, it gives us the key to entering into the Christological and, even more deeply, the Trinitarian, foundation of the priesthood. For the word "servant" expresses the priest's "relativity" to the person of Christ and, at the same time, Christ's "relativity" to the Father. But "servant" also unveils, albeit in an extremely condensed way, the ecclesiological foundation of the priesthood, inasmuch as it bespeaks the priest's "relativity" to the people he serves. For all of these reasons, ever since I realized what the word really means—perhaps reading Saint Augustine encouraged this preference in me—I have felt that it is extremely important for understanding what I have experienced in my priestly life.

Servant of Christ, Servant of the Father

The aim of these reflections, then, is to develop this triple theme: the Trinitarian, Christological, and ecclesiological foundation of the word "servant" as it applies to the ministerial priesthood. Cardinal Ratzinger, speaking at the 1995 symposium marking the 30th anniversary of *Presbyterium Ordinis*, made this topic the center of his whole presentation[3]. The Council document says that priestly identity has an essentially relational character[4], and Ratzinger notes that the term "servant" is precisely a relational one: you are a servant in relation to another. "If the priest is defined as a servant of Jesus Christ, this means that his existence is essentially relational. . . . He is a servant of Christ and then, from him, with him, and through him, a servant of men"[5].

The word "servant" indicates, then, a relation to Christ, whch Ratzinger explains by means of a reflection on the priestly "character." What is the meaning of this indelible character that is impressed on the person of the priest at his ordination? The answer is his "relativity" to Christ. His relativity to Christ for a task. The priestly character means

[3] See Joseph Ratzinger, "Il ministero e la vita dei presbiteri," in *Studi Cattolici* 423 (May 1996): 324-332.
[4] See *Presbyterium Ordinis*, 12.
[5] Joseph Ratzinger, "Il ministero," 327.

that, from this moment on, the ordained man no longer belongs to himself, can no longer do with himself as he pleases, because his life is henceforth the pathway for an initiative that comes from Christ[6]. The priest is "captured" by Christ for a task that Christ wishes to entrust to him: for a specific, particular, task, which the priest must then discover.

There is a deep analogy between the baptismal character and the priestly character. No one can declare that he belongs to Christ on his own initiative, no one can baptize himself, one can only *be* baptized. Similarly, no one can simply decide on his own to be a priest. The Church's authority has to recognize and confirm one's vocation.

Priests belong to Christ, that is, they are his servants, dispensers of goods not theirs. They are called to give something that they could never give in virtue of themselves alone. What priests give does not come from them: not the words they say, not the acts they perform, not what these acts do and signify. After all, they give the Holy Spirit, they make present Christ's sacrifice, which Christ himself offered in his body and blood. It is Christ who is acting through the priest. Recall the famous words Augustine wrote in the thick of the Donatist controversy: "when Augustine baptizes, it is Christ who baptizes"[7].

The deepest aspect of the priest's relationship with Christ lies in the fact that it represents Christ's relationship with the Father. The priest does not pronounce his own words, but Christ's words. Not his own doctrine, but Jesus'. And Jesus himself first said that his teaching is not his own, but that he has received it from the Father (see Jn 7:16), and that

---

[6] See ibid., 328.
[7] Augustine, *De Baptismo contra Donatistas*, V, 12, 14; VI, 28, 54.

he does not do his own works, but those the Father has commanded him to do (see Jn 8:29)[8].

We cannot, then, really understand the priesthood unless we see it as having to do with Jesus' expression of his identity with the Father: "he who receives me receives him who sent me" (Matt 10:40). Not only that, but he said to his Apostles, "apart from me you can do nothing" (Jn 15:5), even as he said of himself "I do nothing on my own authority" (Jn 8:28). This parallel contains the whole depth of what priesthood is all about.

As Christ is the bearer of a mandate that originates from the Father, so, too, the priest is the bearer of a mission that originates from Christ. Paul explains this with reference to himself in 2 Cor 5:18-20. He describes his ministry with an eye both to God and to his fellow men: "knowing the fear of the Lord, we persuade men; but what we are is known to God" (2 Cor 5:11). He then immediately adds: "for the love of Christ controls us, because we are convinced that one has died for all; therefore all have died. And he died for all, that those who live might live no longer for themselves [this is what we have called "relativity" to Christ] but for him who for their sake died and was raised" (2 Cor 5:14-15). A new identity is at play here: belonging.

But then Paul clarifies that "all this is from God, who through Christ reconciled us to himself and gave us the ministry of reconciliation" (2 Cor 5:18). It was God who reconciled the world to himself through Christ; the initia-

---

[8] This is also the center of Balthasar's entire reflection on the priesthood: see Hans Urs von Balthasar, "Esistenza sacerdotale," in *Sponsa Verbi* (Brescia: Morcelliana, 1972), 363-442; "Sacerdoti della Nuova Alleanza," and "Vivere nel celibato oggi," in *Lo Spirito e l'istituzione* (Brescia: Morcelliana, 1979), 279-329.

tive arises from the Father who works through his Son: "so we are ambassadors for Christ, God making his appeal through us" (2 Cor 5:20). Paul thus also draws an explicit parallel between the mission the Father assigns to the Son and the mission the Son assigns to us: "we beseech you on behalf of Christ, be reconciled to God" (2 Cor 5:20).

Just as Jesus announces a message that he did not think up, but is sent by the Father with a task, in the same way the priest must not bear a word that comes from him, but must be an echo of the Word. Augustine calls the Baptist a prototype of the priest and says that every priest is a *"vox"* of the *"Verbum"*: the *Verbum* remains, the *vox* passes away, but it is necessary so that the *Verbum* can be heard[9]. With this image, Augustine sums up everything that is meant by the priest's relationality to Christ[10].

Servant of the Christian People

I have always been struck by reading the tenth chapter of Matthew, where, from among the larger group of disciples, Christ specifically chooses a smaller number for a particular vocation (Mt 10:1-15). Something that leaps out here is Jesus' demanding affection for his disciples. Jesus wants them to declare their allegiance to him even above their dearest human bonds. At the same time, he gives an unimaginable reward: "but even the hairs of your head are all numbered" (Mt 10:30). Christ loves us personally, down

---

[9] See Augustine, *Sermo* XXXCIII/B.
[10] See L. Giussani, "Il sacerdote di fronte alle sfide radicali della società contemporanea," insert in 30 *Giorni* (1995) 11: 1-4.

to the inmost fibers of our being. He knows even what we don't know about ourselves. The priesthood emerges here as the sign of Christ's personal affection for us, which he expresses by speaking our name. Christ assigns each of us a task within his people: the task he assigns to priests is participation in the ministry whereby he creates, guides, and educates his people.

Understanding chapter ten of Matthew requires reading the last few verses of chapter nine, when Jesus, seeing the crowds, is moved to pity because they are weary and exhausted like sheep without a shepherd: "the harvest is plentiful, but the laborers are few" (Mt 9:37). The mission of the Apostles is born out of compassion. The priest is a sign of Christ's mercy, of the divine mercy that Christ is. Priesthood is an assimilation to the life of Christ, to the person of Christ in his being given for men.

Priests—and they must never forget it—are part of Christ's compassion, and the responsibility that he entrusts them is how he loves them, how he educates them, how he gives their life its final form. It is important to bear in mind that Christ fulfills the priest's life by asking him to give it away. It is through giving myself away that I realize myself. In the words of the Gospel, he who loses himself finds himself, whereas he who tries to keep his own life for himself will lose it (see Lk 9:24).

The self-gift the priest is called to make to the Christian people is summed up in the expression "servus servorum Christi." The "servus Christi" is the baptized person, whose very essence is a matter of being relative to Christ. The expression "servus servorum" began to be applied in an eminent sense to the Pope after a certain point in Church history. But it was at first a description of the priest and of his place in the Church. Just what, then, is this place? Just what is the relationship between the ministerial priesthood and the priesthood of the baptized?

Albert Vanhoye helpfully explains this point in his analysis of a key passage of the First Letter of Peter[11]. Peter, speaking of the people of God, compares it to a building having Christ as its cornerstone, "that living stone, rejected by men but in God's sight chosen and precious" (1 Pt 2:4). Everyone who is part of this people is one of the building-blocks of this edifice, "living stones . . . built into a spiritual house, to be a holy priesthood, to offer spiritual sacrifices acceptable to God through Jesus Christ" (1 Pt 2:5). Peter goes on to add: "you are a chosen race, a royal priesthood, a holy nation, God's own people" (1 Pt 2:9).

The first point that needs underlining is that Peter is speaking to the whole people. It is this people that is the new priest in the world, the heir of Christ's priesthood, the sign of God in the midst of the nations, the sign that all are called to salvation. At the same time, this people is the interepreter of the expectations of the nations, called to point out the path of truth to them. The Christian people performs by its very existence the task of mediating between the peoples of the world and God.

What do the expressions "spiritual priesthood," "spiritual sacrifice," "spiritual edifice" mean? They highlight the fact that the priesthood is no longer about immolating animals in the temple enclosure, but a whole existence animated by the Spirit of God. Baptismal priesthood is the offering of one's own existence. In our daily lives, each one of the baptized begins the New Jerusalem through his work and his affective relationships. The new people begins through the building

---

[11] See A. Vanhoye, *Il sacerdozio della Nuova Alleanza* (Milan: Ancora, 1999), 29-36.

up of a new city in which affective relationships and work are animated by God's Spirit and so raise up the Body of Christ.

In order for this to be possible, our belonging to God in Baptism has to flower in our daily lives. There can, however, be no such flowering without the sacraments and the guidance of the Church. It is thus the priesthood of the baptized itself that makes the ordained priesthood necessary. This means, of course, that the latter is at the service of the former. The priesthood of the baptized is the end, the priesthood of the ordained is a means. It is only a service—but it is an indispensable one. Its task is to represent sacramentally the mediatiorship of Christ, who continually draws men to himself and transforms their lives through penance, Eucharist, and the guidance of the Church.

Vanhoye writes:

> Without the ordained priesthood, the priesthood of the baptized could not come into play. By means of the ordained priesthood, Christ himself exercises his priestly mediation, which is the source of all the graces needed for the exercise of the priesthood of the baptized[12].

The ordained priesthood exists for the sake of the people, as a necessary condition of its existence as such[13].

---

[12] Ibid., 135.

[13] Commenting on the passage in Hebrews that describes Jesus as the "merciful and faithful [=worthy of faith]" high priest (Heb 2:17), Vanhoye once again puts the person of Christ at the heart of what it means to be a priest: "worthy of faith" because endowed with authority with the Father and, at the same time, "merciful" with us. Vanhoye criticizes and corrects the more common translation of "*pistos*" as "faithful," suggesting "worthy of faith" instead. See A. Vanhoye, Il *sacerdozio*, 36-43.

In Christ's School

But what does all of this mean concretely for the priest? In order to answer this question, we need to go back once more to the foundation of the priesthood. The primary, fundamental task of the priestly life is our assimilation to Christ, his wisdom, and his charity. This is the purpose of prayer, of meditation, of study, of the trials Christ sends us, of friendship. The holiness of our lives is nothing other than a living out of what Christ asks of us. It's not in the first instance a matter of how much we fast or how many penitential exercises we perform, but of the "Yes" that we say to what Christ asks of us as his servants.

What the sacrament gives birth to, in fact, is a life fed by relationships, encounters, and, therefore, witness. Paul VI once noted that today's world allows teachers, but it acknowledges them only if they are witnesses[14]. This brings to mind a dialogue I once had with a young friend. He asked me whether, in addition to the task of caring for the Christian people, the priest doesn't also have a special task with regard to atheists or believers in other religions. I answered him that the priest's first task is to serve the Christian people. His first task is to collaborate in the conversion of the Christian people, in its education, because this people is the sign lifted up for all men, whether believers or not, and for all peoples to run to. All are called to membership in this people: God "desires all men to be saved and to come to the knowledge of the truth" (1 Tim 2:4). The priest, then, doesn't have two tasks, one for believers and one for non-believers, but just one. He is called to serve the Christian people, but the horizon of this

---

[14] See Paul VI, *Evangelii Nuntiandi*, 41.

people is the world. After its return from exile, Israel also asked about its mission in the midst of the other peoples. Through Isaiah, God says "it is too light a thing that you should be my servant to raise up the tribes of Jacob and to restore the preserved of Israel; I will give you as a light to the nations, that my salvation may reach to the end of the earth" (Is 49:6). In other words: don't think only of yourself; you have to think about the whole world.

What does it mean to serve the Christian people? The answer to this question has to avoid any sort of reduction of the priestly ministry to a function bestowed by the community, a function that ends up being nothing more than a sociological coordination for guiding, ordering, or promoting the liberation of the community. No, we can serve the Christian people only if we remain always in Christ's school. If we should fail to be permanent disciples, then we can no longer be teachers. Sticking with the image used in First Peter, if our eyes are not continually fixed on Christ's place in the Church as the "cornerstone" (1 Pt 2:6-7), we can no longer recognize the place of the other stones, either. If we do not live out our identification with Christ, the labor of building up his people will end up wearing us out.

The building up of the people occurs so to say only in the space of my relationship with Christ. If I am not constantly reclaiming this space, then I cannot help but place everyone else outside of it. The priesthood is a collaboration with Christ's ministry, and it cannot work outside of a constant relationship with him. Without this constant nourishment, a priest cannot truly and rightly live out his task, the responsibility Christ has entrusted to him. If I am supposed to do something he tells me to do, how can I actually do it if I don't listen to him? I will end up doing my own thing instead. How can I do it if not in his presence, if not with him as the horizon of my attention? I will end up taking people where I want them to go.

Let me add an important observation. Although he knows that Christ has chosen him for an important task, the priest has to be a man among men. He has to be a man among men in terms of the conditions of his life, without seeking privileges or special conveniences for himself. He has to be a man among men also in terms of his passion for everything man experiences, of his ability to listen, to relate, to forgive. We are not a caste, and we must avoid a clerical self-image even if we know that we have been chosen from among men in order to be a sign of the newness of grace in the midst of all people. Chosen from among men, but not separated from their existence, just as Christ was not separated from the existence of other men, but took upon himself the human condition in all its dimensions. We are baptized believers among baptized believers, as Paul says: "not that we lord it over your faith; we work with you for your joy, for you stand firm in your faith" (2 Cor 1:24).

Proclamation and Education

The priest gathers the Christian people first and foremost by proclaiming the truth that is Christ and by celebrating the sacraments, above all the Eucharist. Every Christian is a priest by Baptism, but he cannot live out his priesthood independently of the Eucharist. It is only in the Eucharist, in fact, that the people of the baptized becomes the body of Christ in the offering up of their lives. For this reason, the people of God is not fully present without the Eucharist.

Looking at the Eucharist, we understand the priest's other task, which is to educate the people. For the Eucharist is the manifestation of the form God has given to the world, and to educate means precisely to help others recognize the form God has given to their lives. The new world is born from the Cross, and the Eucharist is the contemporaneousness of the Cross. It is the beginning of the new world, which draws men to itself, invites them to conversion, and moves them to seek Baptism. As a sacrifice, that is, as a memorial of the Passion, the Eucharist accomplishes a new birth, a *metánoia*, an inner change, a passing over, a pasch. At the same time, the Eucharist is communion because the presence of Christ's sacrifice on the Cross unites God and man. The whole liturgy is therefore a privileged place for education: in the Eucharist, the beginning of the new creation appears visibly and unambiguously. Indeed, the liturgy incorporates words, things, colors, smells, the senses, the whole bodily dimension in a redeemed unity that makes all of its components an inchoate expression of what lasts for eternity. Only Christianity, the religion of God made man, heals the terrible split between matter and spirit, reason and history, present and future, individual and people, sense knowledge and intellectual knowledge.

A few years ago I visited museums in Tunis and Carthage. I was struck by the mosaics, some Christian and some pagan, which go back to the period between the second and fourth centuries a.d. All of the mosaics are done in the same (Hellenistic) style and have the same themes: flowers, animals, people. But, whereas the pagan mosaics showed nameless divinities, the Christian ones contained many names: the name of a child in a tomb mosaic, the names of the people who had lived in a certain house, the name of a famous bishop, the names of people who are otherwise totally unknown to us. A few centuries later, everything was swallowed up by Islam, and now there are no longer either faces or names.

Here, then, is the point: education is, first and foremost, a great respect for the event that is taking place in the other. Education is the art of helping the other mature to his full stature. In this sense, one cannot be an educator unless one continually allows oneself to be educated in turn, unless education is a fact that wounds me in this very moment through the Church and, in particular, through the environment, the company, that I have recognized as the locus and support of my vocation.

One of the biggest discoveries I have made since the beginning of the priestly Fraternity of which I am the founder and superior[15] is just this originality of each person whom Christ has called together with me: there is no face that God has made that is the same as any other, just as there is no flower, or blade of grass, or "I" that is the same as any other. This is a manifestation of the very mystery of God one and three: with the other members of the Fraternity I have seen how, in the event where their "I" comes into its own, they become one with the others, recognizing the "You" that makes them be. This, for me, is the Church; this, for me, is the priestly Fraternity that I live as an echo of the Church—the place of the event in which "I," my personal originality, comes into its own.

---

[15] The Priestly Fraternity of the Missionaries of Saint Charles Borromeo was recognized by the Holy See as a society of apostolic life of pontifical right in 1999. It originates from the charism of the ecclesial movement Communion and Liberation. The 120 missionaries who are its members live in houses scattered in 20 countries around the world.

But what is the biggest obstacle that keeps our belonging to the Church, or to any genuine Christian community, from becoming a truly educative event? The refusal to accept that, in order to affirm my "I," I have to let it die. The more you flail in fear of drowning, the quicker you will go under; the more you try to hold something back for yourself, the quicker you will really lose it without hope of recovery. What you hold back, the part of you that you hold back, becomes the very thing that kills you in the end.

Either everything is born anew by a "Yes," or else it dies by a "No," by a voluntary estrangement. Think of Perpetua and Felicity, two child martyrs who were put to death on the beach at Tunis (there is a grave on the site of their martyrdom): their eternal stature, the eternal greatness associated with their names, is based on the "Yes" that they pronounced. When Augustine died, there were about 300 Catholic bishops in North Africa; 250 or 300 years later there was nothing left. Everything in the Church, like everything in man, lives or dies in the secret heart of the "I." That is where salvation happens; that is the point where either everything gathers together again . . . or everything ends.

The Grandeur of the Priesthood

I would now like to put myself in the shoes of someone preparing for the priesthood and answer the following question: what is so great about the priesthood? How can it contribute to the happiness and the human fulfillment of the person who lives it out?

I have already said that God has called us to the priesthood in order to reveal to us the face he has intended for us from all eternity, as he imagined us and desired us with the body that we have, with our particular temperament, through the parents who gave us life, in the times and places of concrete, everyday life. For God, "priest" has always been what I look like.

Many of the great men whom God calls in the Bible display an acute awareness of this. Consider the dialogue with Yahweh in which the Prophet Jeremiah receives his vocation. "'Before I formed you in the womb I knew you, and before you were born I consecrated you; I appointed you a prophet to the nations.' Then I said, 'Ah, Lord God! Behold, I do not know how to speak, for I am only a youth.' But the Lord said to me, 'Do not say, 'I am only a youth'; for to all to whom I send you you shall go, and whatever I command you you shall speak" (Jer1:5-7).

Isaiah shows the same conviction: "The Lord called me from the womb, from the body of my mother he named my name. He made my mouth like a sharp sword, in the shadow of his hand he hid me; he made me a polished arrow, in his quiver he hid me away" (Is 49:1-2).

In other words, God conceived me together with the task that he was to entrust to me and the place that he was to assign me in his Church. Saint Paul knew that he had been chosen from his mother's womb and that God had graciously called him to proclaim the Gospel in the midst of the nations (see Gal 1:15-16). And David prayed: "For thou didst form my inward parts, thou didst knit me together in my mother's womb. . . . Thou knowest me right well. . . . Thy eyes beheld my unformed substance; in thy book were written, every one of them, the days that were formed for me, when as yet there was none of them" (Ps 139:13-14; 16).

If, then, this is the face God has always thought of me with, then the only reasonable choice is to adhere to it with understanding, asking God what he wants of me, and with passion, asking for the creative freedom that characterizes the conquered lover. The way to the priesthood will be the way of my happiness only if it is also the way of my freedom, that is, of my intelligent, continual, passionate, sacrificing, cheerful commitment to Christ. "Come and see" (Jn 1:39): this method, which Jesus prescribes at the very same time that he calls people to himself, is the only suitable one for recognizing the truth of the call to the priesthood.

God chooses in order to send. Every vocation comes with the mission of bearing witness to the world that without Christ, life is pointless, but also that a full life is present and is offered to all men through the holy people that is the Church. Paul writes: "I appeal to you therefore, brethren, by the mercies of God, to present your bodies as a living sacrifice, holy and acceptable to God, which is your spiritual worship" (Rom 12:1). In this new sacrifice, every existence, in all of the details that make it up—especially work and one's affective relations—lives already in time in the eschatological world and cries out to men: "You, too, come, if you want to meet a true humanity, right in the midst of our human fragility!"

But Paul adds: "so we, though many, are one body in Christ, and individually members one of another, having gifts that differ according to the grace given to us" (Rom 12:5-6). What, then, is the gift entrusted to us by means of the priestly ministry? It is the gift of being called to be speaking continually of Jesus, of his life on earth, of the great things that he has said and done, so that others may know that his life continues in the present, that he still works, indeed, that his works now are even greater than they were then (see Jn 14:12). It is a high privilege to be prophets, proclaimers, evangelizers, who do not merely heap up empty words, but speak of what they have seen and heard (see Acts 4:20; 1 Jn 1:3). "For I decided," Paul writes, "to know nothing among you except Jesus Christ and him crucified" (1 Cor 2:2).

All of this requires silence, a pure gaze, and a passion for communicating. Jesus entrusts this task to all his followers, but to his priests he says, "you will have no more important goal than this, you will have no business that can exempt you from it or push it into the background. I beg you: even if every other voice should fall silent, let yours at least be heard. I have chosen you for this, for this I have prepared and sent you (see Jn 15:16). Speak in favorable moments, but also in unfavorable ones, because it will not be long before there are no more favorable moments (see 2 Tim 4:2-4). Go, be my voice, not only in Church, not only in the temple precincts, but everywhere, from the rooftops to the basements, in the cities and towns (see Mt 10:27). Do not be afraid, the Spirit will tell you what you are to say, especially when you are mistreated or derided on my account (see Lk 2:11-12; 21:15)."

Priests are not just proclaimers. They are also the servants of the body of Christ through the gift of the sacraments, especially of Confession and the Eucharist. Faced with this fact, not only our mind, but our whole spirit, our whole person, sinks into confusion, even, almost, into discouragement. Why me? Who am I, wretch that I am, to be called to be a privileged servant of Christ's mercy, which these two sacraments sprung from the Cross and the Resurrection display in the highest possible way? It is just here that we see the sublime greatness of the ministry the Church entrusts to us: we are fragile bearers of a treasure whose transmission has been put in our trust (see 2 Cor 4:7). And yet, without men who can say "I absolve you," or "this is my body," men prepared for just this by the Church, this immense treasure would never be given over or handed on.

With that, we touch once more upon the affection and predilection that Jesus has for the priests of his Church, who dispense the most precious goods that he has left to his followers. Once we see this, our dismay turns into emotion and enthusiasm. If you, Jesus, have chosen me, have chosen us, whom you know all too well, it's because you set great store by the celebration of the sacraments, the guiding of prayer, the building of the bridge between heaven and earth—which is what the priesthood *is*. So much so that not only does our weakness not deter you, but it makes you want to accept us, it becomes all the more clear that we are only channels of a forgiveness and of a grace that are yours.

Finally, Jesus has not called us only to be proclaimers and dispensers of the sacraments of his life. He has also called us to be educators, that is, fathers. From the Pope on down to the last priest, all of us, even though we will have no natural children of our own, are chosen to be fathers, that is, men who beget and educate. The world needs fathers, and Christ wants us to be "fathers" whose main concern is to be a refraction of the One who gave us being and provided us with light that we might live and understand, who saved us from nothingness, and who opened to us the doors of the greatest adventure: being forgiven. We are called to meet men everywhere without fear, to accompany them on their way through life, to give them the eyes without which everything looks dark and dull. We are called to be able to open our arms widely enough to embrace even the sick, the old, the children, the abandoned, the dying, because we know that they are the beginning of the revelation of the glorious life that never passes away.

Priestly Formation

I have insisted repeatedly that being an educator requires the willingness to go on being educated in one's own turn. This willingness is a *habitus* that one learns above all in one's seminary years and that one grows ever more deeply into throughout one's whole life. What are the basic channels of this education?

First of all, prayer. Without prayer, no one can have a living personal relationship with Christ. On the other hand, we mustn't confuse prayer with our feeling about prayer. There are moments in our life when prayer seems easy and desirable, and there are also moments—and they can last for years or decades—when prayer can seem toilsome, empty, and arid. There is no reason either to be too happy about the first situation or to be too worried about the second, because feeling is a means whereby God educates us to what matters. When we say morning prayer, we say it even when our head is someplace else, even when we would rather be elsewhere. The prayer that the Church enjoins on its priests has a pedagogical value: it brings us back over and over again to the domain of memory. I recall long stretches of my own life when the thought of the breviary was terrifying: during the first few years after my ordination, I felt a kind of repugnance towards it, and anything would seem more interesting than the Office. On the other hand, there have also been times when the breviary was one of the greatest consolations of my day. I don't know which of the two carries more weight with God: the important thing is for education in memory to continue as a constant thread.

The Gospel often shows us Jesus praying to his Father. Jesus' prayer has always been, for me, one of the most elusive and, at the same time, fascinating mysteries of his existence. Most elusive, because one cannot help asking why Jesus needed to pray, why he needed silence, since, being God, he could go directly to the mystery of the Father; most fascinating, because Jesus' prayer reveals just how deeply he knew what it meant to be a man and shows, at the same time, his trepidation before the most decisive moments of his earthly drama.

The priest is a man of prayer: in prayer he lives out his relationship with Christ and in prayer he brings before Christ those who have been entrusted to him. Above all when he recites the breviary and celebrates Mass, his voice is the voice of other men that becomes a cry to God, that becomes supplication, invocation, a request for forgiveness—all through his voice. In the next life, we will see the threads, which now are invisible to us, that tie all lives, all moments together. This is why the priesthood requires complete availability with respect to one's self, one's time, one's own life—why, in short, it requires virginity. Virginity, in fact, is total availability for men and for the world, and its goal is that their question, their expectation, their entreaty may be brought up to God's altar through the person of the priest and the sacrament that he celebrates. The priest is truly Moses who raises his hands between heaven and earth; he is Abraham who entreats God for salvation (see Ex 9:33; 17:11; Gen 18:20-23). The priest, then, is also called to participate personally in Christ's sacrifice, in an unpredictable, ultimately mysterious, way. He enables men to be reconciled with God, and so is truly a "pontiff," one who intercedes for the unity of the people. For a people is reborn through a reconciliation, that is, a forgiveness, the reception of mercy. Everyone contributes to this new creation with the drama of his own existence.

The priest is also someone who educates to prayer. The liturgy—for years the fundamental experience of my own life—offers an extraordinary education in prayer. The heart of the liturgy is a sacramental event, that is, a fact by means of which God himself forms history. It is this that the celebrant has to bring out. Fr. Giussani taught me to live the liturgy soberly: the celebrant mustn't impose himself on the liturgy, nor must he simply disappear, either. Everything must have its place, and no other: the tone of the voice, the tone of the singing, the untheatrical, but also unslovenly, gestures.

A second basic path of priestly formation is study. After all, the priest is the servant and the herald of the truth. His job is to remove the veil that covers men's eyes, so that they can see what has happened and what is happening. For this reason, the priestly life cannot develop without silence, because without silence the priest cannot penetrate into truth. Anything we communicate that isn't born of silence will be no more than superficial opinions.

We cannot be servants of the truth unless we are students of it. People who are killed by busy-ness no longer meditate, no longer study, no longer reflect. They therefore don't prepare their Sunday homily, they don't prepare the celebration of the sacraments, they don't meditate on what the liturgy has to say. They are on their way to becoming bored and boring, disappointed and disappointing repeaters of themselves.

Speaking of study, I would like to point out that theology springs from the life of the Church: without this ecclesial subject, theology does not exist. When it is ignored, theology becomes philosophy of religion, or it disintegrates into a series of juxtaposed historical, philosophical, and practical disciplines (such as pastoral studies).

As Cardinal Ratzinger points out in an important speech, a theologian has to be enormously cultured, but theology has to be able to jettison dead weight and concentrate on the essential; it has to be able to distinguish between knowing details and knowing the basics; it has to present an organic vision of the whole. When specialized study produces a heap of unrelated details, it has lost its purpose. It is only when we see the whole that we can recognize the indispensable criteria[16]. If we don't learn to judge in the light of the whole, then we will be helpless victims of the latest trends. The Church has always held that one cannot study theology as one studies any other profession. To do so would be like treating the Word of God as our possession, which it isn't. Moses had to remove his sandals before the burning bush. All of the major crises in the history of the Church were essentially bound up with the decadence of the clergy, which no longer experienced their relationship to the Sacred as something thrilling and dangerous, as a searing nearness to the all-holy One—but as an easy way to make a living.

Study is the knowledge of Christ, and it is impossible to know Christ without knowing the history of the Church. Christ is a living man, and Christianity is his body in history. If we were to stop in 33 a.d., we would not meet Christ. We would meet the beginning of Christ, but not Christ. It is a mistake to claim, as some people do, that the only thing

---

[16] See J. Ratzinger, *Cantate al Signore un canto nuovo* (Milan: Jaca Book, 1996), 205.

that should remain in the Church is Christian life as it was in the earliest days. This would be like stopping the flow of a life, fixing its first heart-beats in an idyllic memory. It would also be a mistake to object, for example, that priestly celibacy was not clear when Jesus ascended to the Father. Of course it wasn't, but Jesus didn't stop living; he continued to speak and to give the Church good advice! God, in becoming man, adapts himself lovingly to man's temporal condition. So if we study the history of the Church out of a real interest in knowing Christ, we can learn major lessons from it.

Finally, I want to speak of a third essential aspect of the path to the priesthood, one that makes the seminary years even more decisive for priestly formation: the enormous educational tool known as common life. When Ratzinger was named Bishop of Munich, he found that the seminary had been closed. He wanted to re-open it and so had the building re-built. When it came time to lay the first stone, he instructed that the words of Saint Peter that I cited above should be inscribed on it: "and like living stones be yourselves built into a spiritual house, to be a holy priesthood, to offer spiritual sacrifices acceptable to God through Jesus Christ" (1 Pt 2:5).

What is a "spiritual house"? The most apt point of comparison that I can find is the family. The seminary is a place where people who were originally strangers to one another become family. But their familiarity is a spiritual one, a familiarity that does not arise from flesh and blood, but from the Holy Spirit. Speaking of the priestly Fraternity which I belong to, I can go even further and say that this experience of getting a new family is born of a charism, in the specific meaning of the word. The reciprocal belonging that flows from the Holy Spirit is deeper, stronger, more alive than a simple blood relationship. Men gathered by the touch of the Holy Spirit are close to one another in a way that no other kinship could bring about.

What is this familiarity? It is familiarity with Christ, the fact of having been made Christ's family. Ratzinger points out that Peter, in the above cited passage, says "like living stones *be built*." He does not say "you are" living stones. When the Holy Spirit makes us "become" Christ's family, a passage takes place in our lives. If we want to become a house, we have to accept the fact that we will be worked over; in order to be fitted to the edifice, we have to take on the form that matches the place we will be assigned. If you want to become a stone in the whole, you have to agree to be tied to the whole, and you can't simply do what you want or what seems like a good idea to you. You can't simply go where you want. You have to allow another to gird you and take you where you don't want to go (see Jn 21:18) or, as John says elsewhere, you have to let yourself be carried (see Jn 15:2).

Ratzinger notes that the plan whose accomplishment we desire justifies the torment of pruning and guarantees that we are being purified, not destroyed. In this house we try to grow by learning "whatever is true, whatever is honorable, whatever is just, whatever is pure, whatever is lovely, whatever is gracious, if there is any excellence, if there is anything worthy of praise" (Phil 4:8). We become fitted to this house by becoming true. If this is the goal it is pursuing, then the seminary becomes a home; if it doesn't take this path, then it is just a bunch of rooms for students, and their occupants remain alone with themselves. The readiness to be purified is the thing that guarantees good cheer and joy in a home. If this readiness is missing, the result is a pervasive climate of ill-humor, of dissatisfaction with everything and with oneself, where the days are gray and joy can't grow because it lacks the sunlight it needs to spread its branches[17].

If we agree to be formed, then the true locus of the priesthood is born: not a temple made of stones, but the temple that is the body of Christ, the place where God dwells, that is, the space where he is present in this world.

Excursus: A Reading of *Presbyterium Ordinis*

Two documents of the Second Vatican Council are devoted to the priesthood: one to priestly formation, *Optatam Totius*, the other to priestly life, *Presbyterium Ordinis*. I would like to propose a brief account of the first chapter ("The Presbyterate in the Mission of the Church") and the first section of the second chapter ("The Ministery of Presbyters") of *Presbyterium Ordinis*. My aim will be to identify the essential elements of the foregoing discussion of the priesthood in the Council's document.

Presbyterium Ordinis points out that the Lord himself promoted to the ministry some of those whom he had called to follow him. Jesus' will is thus at the origin of the priesthood: the initiative comes from him. He promoted some of his followers to the ministry to make them "able by the sacred power of orders to offer sacrifice and to forgive sins"[18]. The Council then adds: "the same Lord, however, has established ministers among his faithful to unite them together in one body"[19]. This, then, is the purpose: the creation, the

---

[17] See ibid., 195.

[18] PO, 2.

[19] Ibid.

regeneration, of the people of God. The ordained ministry, then, makes sense only as something relative to Christ as its origin and to the body of the Church and its unity as its goal.

A second important point that the document highlights is that the priesthood is a participation in the community of the Apostles. It is, we could say, the continuity of the Apostles in time. Jesus' act of creating the ordained ministry implies that the Apostles, in their turn, extended to others what they had received from him. "Therefore, having sent the Apostles just as he himself had been sent by the Father, Christ, through the Apostles themselves, made their successors, the bishops, sharers in his consecration and mission. The office of their ministry has been handed down, in a lesser degree indeed, to the priests"[20]. We can identify the beginning of apostolic succession already in the letters of Saint Paul. Right from the start, the Church was concerned about the transmission to others of the authority it received from Christ. "Receive the Spirit," Jesus says after his Resurrection, before going on to add: "if you forgive the sins of any, they are forgiven" (Jn 20:23). We also find him saying "do this in remembrance of me" (Lk 22:19) and "go into all the world and preach the gospel to the whole creation" (Mk 16:15).

The Council uses three important verbs: the presbyterate participates in the authority by which Christ "builds up, sanctifies, and rules his Body".[21] In this context, *Presbyterium Ordinis* speaks of the priestly character, which configures priests to "Christ the Priest in such a way that they can act in the person of Christ the Head"[22]. *Lumen Gentium* 10 also reiterates this character-theology. The first paragraph of

---

[20] Ibid.

[21] Ibid.

[22] Ibid.

Presbyterium Ordinis offers a synthetic panorama of what it will go on to develop in the rest of the document: the priestly life displays itself through the apostolic proclamation of the Gospel and through the sacrifice of Christ who perfects the spiritual sacrifice of the faithful. Note how the document always relates the Eucharist to the spiritual sacrifice of the faithful, that is, to the life of Christ's Body.

Third, the Council expresses the priest's educative task with the term "govern." The purpose of this "governance" is to enable believers, "working freely and with a grateful spirit," to receive the faith that is proclaimed and accomplished in the Eucharist, so that man's whole life might be transformed into an offering to "the glory of God the Father in Christ"[23].

The following number deals with a subject that is dear to me, and which I have touched upon above: priests are men among men, as the Letter to the Hebrews puts it: "ordained for men in the things that belong to God in order to offer gifts and sacrifices for sins, [they] nevertheless live on earth with other men as brothers"[24]. They live among their fellow men, because this is the condition to which Jesus has called them and that Jesus chose for himself. The fact that they live among men as their brothers is an imitation of Christ. At the same time, priests are "by a special title" forbidden to "be conformed to this world"[25], to identify with its mentality, even though they remain among their fellow human beings.

In numbers 4, 5, and 6, the document deals with the presbyteral ministry, that is, with the tasks entrusted to priests. First of all, priests have a prophetic responsibility:

---

[23] Ibid.

[24] Ibid., 3. See Heb 5:1.

[25] Ibid.

"the People of God," the document states, "are joined together primarily by the word of the living God. And rightfully they expect this from their priests"[26]. This statement is a solemn one: priests must not speak their own words, but must be an echo of Christ who is Wisdom. The people of God has a right to receive this wisdom, and not just human wisdom, from priests. The Council is recalling here the fact that faith is born of hearing, and that no one can be saved without faith (see Mk 16:15-16). This is an echo of Jesus' urgent invitation: "go into all the world and preach the gospel to the whole creation" (Mk 16:15). Balthasar and Ratzinger show how the Council's teaching on the priest's prophetic task includes an invitation to action[27]. The Gospel never divides Jesus' words from his actions; it always presents these actions as the summit of his prophetic office. On the other hand, the word that the priest is called to proclaim is the "word of the living God," the word of God-made-man. The Council wants to reaffirm that the primary task of the priesthood is the proclamation of the faith and that it is absolutely necessary for the priest to dedicate himself to the study of the Word of God, also in its literal, historical aspect, so that he may unceasingly ponder it and penetrate its depths. The priest is not a professor of exegesis. It is only by continually identifying himself with the person of Christ, which comes to us also through the saving word of Scripture, that the priest finds his nourishment and discovers how to communicate to his fellow men. The Council cites Jesus' claim in John's Gospel that "the word which you hear is not mine" (Jn 14:24) and says quite clearly that the

---

[26] Ibid., 4.
[27] Hans Urs von Balthasar, "Sacerdoti," 295-303; Joseph Ratzinger, "Il ministero," 326.

priest must not teach a wisdom of his own, but the wisdom that he has received: "they are relying not on their own wisdom, for it is the word of Christ they teach, and it is to conversion and holiness that they exhort all men"[28].

It seems to me that today the prophetic task is the most important of all those entrusted to the presbyterate. In a time like ours, when half the world does not know who Christ is and the half that does denies or forgets him, the most urgent task is prophecy. This is the first task of every Christian. In a certain sense, the entire point of the Church is prophecy. As Jesus says, "You are a city set on a hill a lamp on a stand" (see Mt 5:14-15). Prophecy, the proclamation that Christ is present as the world's judge, is not necessarily expressed in words. In the Old Testament, Yahweh often commands the prophets to perform symbolic actions or gestures, which they are to carry out along with, or even instead of, words. Clearly, prophecy, even before being something to be said or done, is first and foremost the awareness that one has of being sent by Christ: the awareness of being different from the world, of being ontologically transformed by Baptism, of Christ's presence, of the imminence of his return and his judgment.

Presbyterium Ordinis goes on to describe the priest as a minister of the Eucharist and the other sacraments. Priests are "sharers by special title in the priesthood of Christ"[29], in the sense that Christ has entrusted to them the ministry of his holiness. Citing Thomas, the Council says that the "Most Blessed Eucharist contains the entire spiritual boon of the Church"[30]. The Eucharist is the fulfill-

---

[28] PO, 4.

[29] Ibid., 5.

[30] Ibid.

ment of life and the end of all the sacraments[31]. The priest's task of celebrating the sacraments, where Christ's holiness is communicated, is thus closely united with, and ordered to, the Eucharist, which, as the document goes on to say, is the "source and the apex of the whole work of preaching the Gospel"[32].

For this reason, priests must teach the faithful to offer their own lives in union with the life of Christ, the victim sacrificed in the Mass. By the same token, priests need to educate believers to the sense of the offertory. Praying the blessing over the bread and the wine, the priest says that they are the "fruit of the earth and the work of human hands". The bread and the wine gather up all the paths, all the questions, all the expectations, all the wanderings, all the mistakes of the people present and become, with them, the body and blood of Christ. The document also speaks of the Sacrament of Penance and the other sacraments, while explaining the relationship between priestly life and prayer, and between priestly life and the liturgy[33].

Finally, in the following number, the document develops more fully the way in which the priest is an educator of the people. The priest's educative task has to do with unity. The priest has to gather "the family of God together as a brotherhood enlivened by one spirit", and a special "spiritual power"[34] is bestowed on him for this purpose, so as to make him the teacher and the agent of this unity. His job

---

[31] See Thomas Aquinas, *Summa Theologiae*, III, 73, 3 c.

[32] PO, 5.

[33] See ibid.

[34] Ibid. 6.

is not to organize a mass movement, but to develop the vocation of each of the faithful:

> Priests therefore, as educators in the faith, must see to it either by themselves or through others that the faithful are led individually in the Holy Spirit to a development of their own vocation according to the Gospel, to a sincere and practical charity, and to that freedom with which Christ has made us free. Ceremonies however beautiful, or associations however flourishing, will be of little value if they are not directed toward the education of men and women to Christian maturity[35].

---

[35] Ibid.

II
Obedience

Being Generated

Man is not spiritually fruitful unless he continuously lets himself be generated[36]. This is a decisive point, not only for the life of the priest, but also for the life of the Christian as such. If my life is not moved at every instant, I will never be capable of communication.

These words reveal something even more fundamental, however: without generation, there is no "face". My personal face, my countenance, is given by a generative act that is happening at this very instant. This is a reality that we find expressed already in the Psalms: "if you withdraw, I become dust" (see Ps 104:29). The Spirit is the actuality of the God who creates and saves. Without a conscious and living welcome of God's creating and saving act, my person does not exist.

Now, God's act of creation and salvation reaches me *hic et nunc* through the sacrament that is the Church. And the way in which I most often get involved with the Church is through a small group of persons, a company of my fellow

---

[36] Don Giussani has condensed this profound truth of man's being in one concise phrase: "No one generates unless he is generated." See Luigi Giussani, "Nessuno genera se non è generato," insert in *Tracce—-Litterae Communionis* (1997) 6.

human beings[37]. Such is the method that God himself has chosen: he has decided to communicate himself creatively and redemptively to man through the being and action of a people, of a company. My face is constituted, then, in my relation with a company established by God. This dynamism of communication is in turn the necessary condition enabling my person to contribute to human history.

The greatest gift for our lives is therefore the chance to obey cordially and uncomplicatedly the company in which God generates us at every instant. By placing us in a house, in a small or large community, God fully displays his mercy towards each one of us. After all, so long as the person is not helped along to the discovery of his definitive place in the scheme of things, he cannot truly feel enfolded by the eyes of mercy. Jesus himself teaches us this through the story of the Good Samaritan who picks up the wounded traveler and brings him to a house (Lk 10: 30-34): there is no true charity that is not also ready to welcome the person in a concrete way. This is why Christian holiness always tries to create a human environment where the person can be guided and sheltered.

This gift charges me at the same time with a responsibility. The entire process of growth towards the fulfillment of my person takes concrete shape in a living, intelligent, and passionate adherence to the company that God has chosen as the place in which he generates me. I have selected these three adjectives with care. A "living" adherence, then, means an adherence to a place in which I seek

---

[37] See Luigi. Giussani, "Noi siamo degli ebrei," in *La Repubblica*, 01-02-99: 13; republished in *Tracce—-Litterae Communionis* (1999) 1: 1; now in Luigi Giussani, *L'io, il potere, le opere* (Genoa: Marietti, 2000), 268-270.

who I am and am not content merely to tidy up this or that aspect of my life; it means a dramatic adherence that mobilizes everything that goes to make up my personality. When I describe this adherence as "intelligent," I mean that precisely this dramatic experience of fulfillment that happens in relationship is the context in which I become aware of what is true and my intelligence finds an answer to its thirst. Finally, in speaking of adherence as "passionate," I want to point out that freedom plays a role here, inasmuch as it seizes the true as a definitive good, as the good that quenches my thirst, as a "Thou" who is the answer I have been waiting for. At the same time, the encounter with the good and the true always brings with it the shock of the new, and so a wound. Having said this, we have indicated the twofold meaning of the word "passion."

The company in which God has placed us is therefore a tremendous grace for each one of us. On the other hand, the acknowledgment of this must not remain on the level of a sociological observation. If it is going to be an authentic acknowledgment of the work of God, it has to penetrate to the source of the grace that we recognize, to the root that continually nourishes it. It has to penetrate to the acknowledgment of Christ in his presence here and now in the company that he generates[38]. To keep looking until we see Christ is not something that we do after the acknowledgment of the company as the place where we are generated. Rather, it is the same thing as this recognition; it is the whole that

---

[38] Once again we are guided by the words of Luigi Giussani: "Dare del tu a Cristo" [addressing Christ familiarly]. This is the title under which one of his conversations with a group of Memores Domini was published in 30*Giorni* (1998) 9: 46-55; now in Luigi Giussani, L'*attrattiva Gesù* (Milan: BUR, 1999), 159ff.

provides the horizon in which things find their proper place. From the natural point of view, if we removed this horizon, we could no longer put things in their proper place; we would have something like a painting without perspective. The greatness of the individual thing, of the individual person, is his placement within the whole falling within my field of vision. But this greatness is given by the horizon, by the perspective, by the depth of the gaze that penetrates to the ultimate point from which everything originates.

This train of thought is not complete, however, until we have taken account of Christ's mercy, which is God's own method, and considered how far it reaches. God creates a people, and within this people he creates a network of companionships, of friendships, which meet each of us on his own terrain in order to embrace him from close up. The company that God has created as a place to generate the person is therefore an event of vocation. No one can understand what this sort of company means to him independently of the event of his vocation. The vocation is decided by God. It is God who fixes the place of each person within his people, the function that each person is to exercise for this people. It is he who gives each one of us a name ("you will no longer be Simon, but Cephas"; "you will no longer be Saul, but Paul": see Jn 1:42; Acts 13:9). Vocation is thus the acknowledgment of a new principle of dependence different from the natural family or the social contexts in which a person happens to find himself. This is what St. Francis experienced when gave even the clothes he was wearing back to his father in Assisi and declared that he would no longer say "my father," but "Our Father who art in heaven"[39].

---

[39] See "La leggenda dei tre compagni," in *Fonti francescane* (Assisi: Movimento Francescano, 1978), 1081f.

I would like to develop three brief remarks on this point. First of all, it is impossible to preserve the recognition of a new principle of dependence without silence in one's life. When chatter, when talk gains the upper hand during the day, it squeezes out silence that listens to the work of God. The poet Clemente Rebora once wrote: "your word silenced my chatter" [*la tua parola zittì chiacchiere mie*][40]. Silence is listening to the voice of God. It is not the absence of talking, but active listening to the voice that is most interesting to me. Silence is an opportunity to perceive the work of God operating in the depths. If there is no silence, we would perceive only the surface, the crust of this work. Without silence, everything becomes journalism, a newspaper story. Silence is of course prayer, so long as we do not understand prayer as a pious practice, but as a living awareness of being generated, of being made here and now, and thus also as a request for being, just as it is a request for what we need.

The second observation is that we are always in need of recovering the awareness of Christ as the origin of the human company of which we are members. This is where those who hold the position of educators and authorities in this company help us. If we lose the reference to the origin of our being together, our common life becomes a purely extrinsic, sociological fact. Conversely, if we lose sight of the concrete face of the brother who is placed beside us, we fall into spiritualism. This is why, when Jesus was asked "which is the greatest commandment?" he answered "love God, love your neighbor" (see Mt 22:36-39). Not just the one or the other, but both.

---

[40] Clemente Rebora, "Curriculum Vitae," in *Le Poesie* (Milan: All'insegna del Pesce d'Oro, 1982), 285.

The third observation: sharing life with the brothers who have been called along with me requires a gift of self without measure. We must therefore continually purify the awareness with which we live out this gift lest it become a form of voluntarism. We therefore have to be vigilant in order to make sure that we always keep in view the ultimate reason why we are together. When we do that, we will be able to break through the screen that our weaknesses are constantly creating between us and the ideal. We are enabled to start again at every instant, beyond jealousy, envy, rivalry, pettiness, and mutual exclusion.

Handing Oneself Over

Christ promised those who followed him with their whole being a "hundredfold" (see Mk 10:30). This promise can be fulfilled in our lives only if we can get to the point of accepting God as a mystery. This is the first and fundamental form of obedience. But the words "God is a mystery" can sometimes be just a phrase that we mouth but that does not mean anything. The Mystery can hit us unexpectedly like a fist in the stomach, can force us on our knees, make us weep. For this reason, it is not an option for us to assume an aesthetic attitude towards the statement that "God is a mystery." The mystery of God has manifested itself in the death of the Son hanging on a cross! That the Only-begotten Son of God, who is coeternal with the Father, could nonetheless cry out "why have you abandoned me?" (Mk 15:34) is something that totally escapes our comprehension. What an abyss of otherness, of trial, comes to expression in those words!

Unless we perceive the presence of the Mystery in our own lives, we have no chance of finding peace and of truly becoming who we really are. But the word "perceive" is not yet sufficient. We have to take a step further and speak of "adherence" to the Mystery. And what does it mean to adhere to the Mystery? We should know by now that it is not simply a matter of pious feelings, but is something extremely concrete. It means to adhere to the company, the human milieu, that he has created for us and in which he manifests himself as our Redeemer. God has become man. By the same token, he has chosen the same law for his self communication: he comes to us through the human. If we do not accept this law, we cannot live out our relationship with him. All of this is dramatic, because the Mystery that we adore appears under fragile wrappings. His divinity conceals itself behind his humanity, even as it reveals itself through it.

With his Passion just around the corner, Jesus brings his Apostles to the Temple and shows them a poor lonely widow who casts a few small coins into the treasury, while others offer gold coins from what they have to spare. Jesus praises her because she has given everything (see Mk 12:41-44). Why does Jesus do this before dying and rising? In order to impart an essential lesson to his disciples: "you can follow me only with your whole heart." You cannot depend on him "partly," follow him "in some things," belong to him "just so far and no further."

The thing that makes our lives great is not the absence of limits or of mistakes in ourselves and in those around us, but the total integrity with which we hand ourselves over to Christ through the concreteness of the place in which he embraces us. Limits and mistakes will never be lacking because we will always be stumbling. The secret of life is thus essentially a matter of belonging to Christ with one's whole self, just as one is, without any reservations.

I'm reminded here of the words of a song: "E*t le poids de tes péchés eux-mêmes/ te ramènerait Jérusalem"* [even the weight of your sins/ would lead you back, Jerusalem][41]. Even the weight of your sins, Jerusalem, would lead you back to me, God says. The whole of Christian wisdom is summed up in this sentence. For in becoming man, God chose to communicate himself, not only in spite of fragility, but "through" it. If we agree to this divine method without reservation, we can stop looking at our limitations as a reason for discouragement or frustration, and so as something to forget, to censor, and can start looking at them as stones to build with. The whole of our lives, with all their lights and shadows, exists in order to manifest the glory of Christ (see Jn 9: 3). If we refuse this logic, life will always be a burden that sooner or later we will find unbearable.

We are frequently tempted to censor difficulties, to hide them even from ourselves. When we do that, we are diverging radically from the way that God acts with us: every detail is a matter of importance for him. This kind of censorship is a diabolical act, which is often born of a fear of another's judgment, of the fear of losing the positive image that others have of us. But our stature before Christ has nothing to do with this image, nor can it be measured in terms of the mistakes that we may make or avoid making.

---

[41] A.M. Cocagnac, "Chant de pénitence: '*Oh, si tu savais combein je t'aime,/tu retournerais Jérusalem!/Et le poids de tes péchés eux-mêmes/te ramènerait Jérusalem'* [oh, if you knew how much I love you / you would come back, Jerusalem / even the weight of your sins / would lead you back, Jerusalem], in *Canti biblici di padre* A.M. *Cocagnac*, supplement to *Tracce—Litterae Communionis* (1999) 1: 14f.

Rather, it is decided by Christ himself and by our belonging to him. So to hide your own limits, your own problems, really doesn't make any sense. You do not find freedom from your own miseries by censoring them, but by handing them over to Christ, which is to say, by letting him embrace them. This embrace is like the one with which the mother enfolds her child in her arms, with which the lover takes the beloved into his. Indeed, it is infinitely more affectionate than these other gestures. Within this embrace, everything is taken up and directed to the one goal that makes life exciting: the glory of Christ on earth.

Fatherhood as Obedience to the Other

The heart of the mystery of the Incarnation, which is the mystery of Christ's act of handing himself over to us is this: God wants to communicate himself through the human, and he accepts all of its ambiguities. God enters into the problematic complexity of our existence in order to make it shine transparently with his light.

The realization that God has chosen to meet me where I am through something human implies a great responsibility on my part. Loving actual persons is an adventure that never ends. There never comes a time in my responsibility as a brother, a father, or a friend when I can say "well, now we're OK, we have solved all of our problems, now we can relax." Every person is a living reality: some day a new aspect of his personality will come to light, and it will be our task to welcome it responsibly.

A mature belonging to the company in which we live out our vocation requires this type of obedience: obedience to the other as he is, moment by moment. We acquire this capacity to love the other gradually, through trials, difficulties, and exhilarating discoveries. For this reason, a responsible friendship requires patience, it requires the ability to accept and accompany the other. In an authentic Christian company, every relationship is a mutual education. No one is the master of the other, not even of a single aspect of his personality. We are nothing but servants of what God creates.

On the other hand, the act of welcoming the person of the other as a given is the first step towards his education. This is why the task of education is in every case such a delicate business: we need to be able to accept the other in every aspect of his being, which can appear in different lights over time, and to help him along the path towards the full realization of himself. The thing that is most helpful to the other is the daily, objective, physical presence of someone welcoming and patient who, without making any great claims for himself, reveals to him that at every moment Christ loves and waits for him with the burden of his problems, his objections, and his reluctance.

God educates me through the things that he makes happen in my life. Giovanni Battista Vico would say that facts are the truth of God[42]. The primary facts are the persons that he sends along my way, together with their particular histories, temperaments, circumstances, and expectations. If these "facts" are to grow according to the will of God into a "well-ordered building" (Eph 2:21), they need to find a father, someone who welcomes what they are and helps it unfold according to the particular voca-

---

[42] G. B. Vico, De antiquissima, I,1, 2.

tion that God has decided for each of them. The most important thing, then, is fatherhood, which guides the other towards the ideal while dealing with his reality as it is.

Common Generation

Our life is relative to God: its purpose is God's glory. Now, being relative to God means being relative to the work that he has created for us: the Church. At the same time, this work grows in our midst and spreads throughout the world by means of what I call a "common generation," the soul of which is a communional experience of oneself. At the basis of common generation, then, is a new conception of oneself as a "we," the awareness that the deepest texture of one's own being is communion. It is in this experience that genuine spiritual fruitfulness becomes a reality for us.

In order to understand the meaning of the phrase "common generation," we need to remember that Christianity is born and spreads in the world by the presence and power of God. The power of God manifests itself through events that establish something new within the world. Our life is therefore authentic and fruitful only if we adhere to what God does.

The fundamental expression of God's power is Jesus Christ, who alone can convert men's minds and hearts. By the energy of his Spirit, he penetrates to the very ontological depths of the persons and things that the Father gives him in order to assimilate them to himself. In this way, he gives shape to his mysterious body, the Church.

From a methodological point of view, two things make the Church present in a particular environment: the perceptible unity of Christians and their connection with authority[43].

The unity of Christians is based on their conscious participation in the sacraments. This participation makes them more and more into a single reality and is the source of a feeling of unity and community governing the whole of life. This feeling, in turn, seeks a perceptible and social expression for the good of the world and of men. This unity is what every human being is waiting for, it is the experience that most corresponds to the deepest desires that every human being carries within himself. If unity is real, if it is not a fragile emotional harmony, if instead it engages freedom to live it out dramatically, it becomes a vehicle of God's power. This is why the priest is called to live in the midst of the people. That is, his task is to contribute to the generation of this unity, to be a conduit of the power of God that is manifested in it.

The authenticity of this unity requires a second factor: a permanent connection with the authority of the Church. In living out its mission, the Christian community takes authority as its constant point of reference. This alone guarantees that the community is truly part of the body of Christ and a vehicle of his redemptive power.

When common generation is seen within this horizon, it becomes clear that it is not a duty to fulfill. To understand it simply as a matter of duty is to fail to grasp the fact that Christ, moved by a total love for us to which we have merely responded, has taken the first step towards us in an absolutely gratuitous way. Every duty-based approach,

---

[43] See Luigi Giussani, "Una grande premessa," in *Appunti di metodo cristiano* (Milan: Gioventù Studentesca, 1964); now in Luigi Giussani, *Il cammino al vero è l'esperienza* (Turin: SEI, 1995),79-82.

moreover, is short-lived. It has no staying power, and almost always ends up in violence.

Common generation is also not a strategy for more effective missionary action. This way of understanding it is mistaken because it rests entirely on self-confidence. By contrast, the root of common generation is the desire that Christ would manifest his redemptive presence through us. He is the origin of our unity and it is through this unity that he enters into the history of men. Our intelligence, our learning, our shrewdness are important, but they are not what makes mission be mission. The awareness of being in the midst of the community with others can never be exhaustively defined by sentiment or by our abilities, but only by something that has happened among us and has changed our lives.

In order that everyone may see more clearly this "Thou" who is in our midst, we may have to sacrifice our own opinions and projects. When St. Paul is required to judge whether or not one ought to eat of the meat sacrificed to idols, he says clearly that the question is in itself unimportant, since the idols do not exist. Nevertheless, he proposes to abstain from meat sacrificed to them in order to avoid scandalizing any of his brothers (see 1 Cor 8 1-13). He thereby teaches us that communion, as an expression of the mystery of Christ's presence, is much more important than our personal opinions. It is clear, then, that common generation is not something one learns how to do and then puts into practice: it is something that requires an education, a continual conversion.

III
Poverty

Possession Redeemed

Someone listening to people talk about poverty might get the idea that it is one particular experience among many that a few members of the Church embrace voluntarily. He might think that it is something that, while fine and praiseworthy, is not necessary to be a Christian.

The first thing that I would like to do in these reflections on poverty is to stress just the opposite. Poverty has to do with, and reveals and nourishes, the novelty that Baptism has brought about in the baptized. In other words, poverty brings us back to the ontology of the person, to the fact of his being one with Christ[44]. So we have to start here if we want to understand what "poverty" means. For poverty, obedience, and virginity are how the new man lives out his relationship with Being and with beings.

Poverty is born from the discovery that I am Another's: I exist because I am loved in an individual way by Another. My being is from first to last totally relative to him, though not without the mystery of my freedom. If I am the work of Another, nothing is mine, because everything is given to me by him. At the same time, however—here is the paradox—everything is mine because I have been given to

---

[44] See Luigi Giussani, *Si può (veramente?!) vivere così?* (Milan: BUR, 1996), 345.

know the purpose for which it exists, a purpose which Jesus revealed at the end of his life: "that they might know you, oh Father, and he whom you have sent" (Jn 17:3). It has been given to me, then, to know the great reason why God made the world. But I have been also asked to live out every relationship and use everything while keeping this reason in mind. This apparent paradox is the locus of the thrilling and fascinating secret of poverty.

Everything has been put into my hands for a positive purpose. To live in the awareness of this fact means to live poverty. Poverty, then, is not something that grinds man down, but something that lifts him up. His relations with things acquire a lightness and a freedom that are otherwise unimaginable. Poverty is the beginning of those "new heavens and new earth" of which St. Peter speaks (2 Pt 3:13), the beginning of a truly human world.

Poverty cannot exist unless it is fed by hope, that is to say, by the certainty that we have been given what really counts in life and that no one can take it away from us. Everything else is accessory and functional: whether you have a hundred books or one book, a hundred pieces of furniture or one, is not what is important. The decisive thing is what we need in order to participate in the kingdom of God and to spread it in the world. The point is not that everything else is no longer valuable. It is just that its usefulness is measured in function of this goal. So you see that poverty is freedom from things, the awareness that it is God who fulfills our desires[45]. If I place the hope of my fulfillment in possessing a certain thing, I am no longer hoping in Christ, but in that thing. If, however, I hope in Christ who gives me that thing, then I am free of it, I am

---

[45]   See Luigi Giussani, *Si può (veramente?!) vivere così?*, 216.

also free to accept that he might take it away from me[46]. No one who has not experienced it for himself can imagine the freedom born of the experience of poverty. This freedom makes it possible to use and enjoy everything without needing anything. St. Paul gives the community at Philippi his own testimony on this point: "I have learned to be rich, I have learned to be poor" (Phil 4:12). But the origin of this freedom is the acknowledgment that one has received an immense gift.

Just as hope is the "constructive" virtue of faith, poverty, too, is a constructive virtue. Hope, in fact, is faith engaged in the building up of the world. It is an "architectonic" virtue. In the same way, poverty, understood as the use of things according to their true purpose, is a virtue for building up, a virtue animated by the certainty that God's promises are being fulfilled. Unless you are certain of having already received everything, in fact, you cannot have the freedom to use what you hold in your hands according to its ultimate purpose. You will be out for your own safety, you will tighten your grip on things, and so you will set the stage for your own destruction.

To be poor, then, is to use each thing according to its ultimate end, placing the expectation of one's good, not in the possession of this or that thing, but in the realization of the kingdom of God. When we do that, we use, appreciate, and love each thing without turning it into an idol. When they become idols, persons and things cease to be ours: they are like objects that irreparably break to pieces

---

[46] "Faith enables me to recognize Christ's presence, I possess Christ, and so I am certain of the future, that is hope. What is opposed to this hope is any of the ways in which man places his hope in some thing determined and chosen by him" (ibid., 215).

in our hands. In a correct relationship with things and with other people, we do not refuse them the esteem that is their due—for example, you do not deny the value of a person if you are friends with him. At the same time, however, one does not expect from them the fulfillment of one's own life. It is in the kingdom of God that things and persons find their proper place.

An experience of this kind is always precarious; you have always just provisionally attained it. You have to ask for it again and again and, in a certain sense, begin it again and again, because we are not able to keep ourselves from falling into idolatry. We need to keep on being reborn and converted. For this reason, there is no way of getting around the fact that the experience of poverty will feel like being stripped of something precious. Poverty is truly the sign of a new birth, the birth of something definitive and eternal, the beginning of the world that does not pass away. But it can be none of these things unless we suffer through the experience of being stretched in the pain of giving birth: "we are—this is the poverty of the Christian man—stretched as it were between the grace that originates us, which gives us a new being, and the manifestation of this new being that we already are"[47].

Through this stripping, however, an endless joy comes to birth. For when we live poverty, we discover that we are lacking nothing, since everything is given to us. Not only are we given everything that we need, but we are assured that it will never be taken away from us, as St. Paul says: "everything is yours, because you are Christ's,

---

[47] Luigi Giussani, *La vita: Dio si è "immischiato con noi"*, insert in *Tracce—Litterae Communionis* (1999) 10: VII.

as Christ is God's" (see 1 Cor 3:22-23). In another passage, the Apostle says that time is grown short (see 1 Cor
7:29): we are already in the definitive hour, the hour in
which, after the Incarnation, death, and Resurrection of
Jesus, we human beings possess everything, but in a new
way.

The Luminousness of Poverty

"Arise, clothe yourself in light, because your light has
come, the glory of the Lord has risen upon you. For behold,
darkness covers the earth, thick cloud covers the nations.
But the Lord shines upon you" (Is 60:1-2). In these words,
the Prophet describes for us the awareness that the Church
ought to have of itself, of what it has received, of what it is,
of what is called to be in the world and for the world: a light
that dispels the darkness, glory shrouded in a fog that it is
nonetheless called to disperse.

This is the real reason why we can and must speak of
the poverty of the Church. By its radiance and beauty,
poverty shows forth the deep nature of Christ's Church.

Think of the medieval cathedrals. People who for the
most part lived in extremely modest houses made of wood
or of mud, who lived in huts, raised up for God a house like
the one at Chartres. Why did they do this? Because they
felt that God's house was made to be a reminder of a full,
beautiful, and luminous life that would make everything
more beautiful—including the fact of going to work,
including the difficulties of family life, including the burden of social conditions.

Today we are called to leave new traces of this beauty.
We are a sign of the presence of Another, which we must-

n't obscure with either pomp or shabbiness. This is why I want the houses where the Missionaries of the Fraternity of St. Charles to be markings of this luminous poverty[48], which not only comes from Christ, but must also be an introduction to him. It must awaken the "suspicion" that a different humanity is possible, as the Prophet Isaiah says: "clothe yourself in light, because your light has come" (Is 60:1).

Education to Poverty

Poverty is the recovery of authenticity in our relationship with things, the authenticity in which God placed man at the dawn of creation and at the dawn of the new creation that is the Resurrection of Christ. To be educated to poverty, therefore, does not mean to be educated to not having. Poverty—let me underscore this again—is not a negative way of looking at life's material goods. Rather, it is a positive way of looking: it is the most positive way of looking that one can have. Poverty teaches us how to use everything without being used by anything, without being slaves of anything: we are "people who have nothing and yet possess everything" (2 Cor 6:10; see also 1 Cor 7:31).

For this reason, poverty can only be total. There is no part-time poverty. Unless you live out poverty in a radical way, you cannot be a sign that fascinates your fellow human beings. But what does it mean to live out poverty in a radical way? It means to be conscious that everything is given for the glory of Christ, including the necessity and duty of seeing to one's own upkeep, of working to earn one's bread. After all, this, too, is an aspect of his glory. St. Thomas says that private property is of divine right, and there is at least one item of private property that must always be safeguarded: one's own body[49].

That having been said, education in living out poverty in a total way takes place gradually. This is true first and foremost because education, as such, is a journey with no end. Furthermore, this is even truer when it comes to dealing with a topic that is as tricky and as important as the issue of possessions and of money. We need to be educated to poverty, then, because otherwise we run the risk of fighting a toilsome battle our whole lives only to die in a minor "skirmish" at the end. How pathetic it is that people get into fights and slit one another's throats for a handful of pennies! And yet, struggle over money has been the cause of numberless tragedies, even in religious institutes. This is why we have to help each other and to learn how not to overburden our life, which is already weighed down by the body as it is: "a corruptible body weighs down the soul," Scripture says (Wis 9:15).

What are the means of this gradual education? In the first place, one cannot live out poverty if one's life does not belong authentically to Christ. One's reluctance to embrace poverty grows as one's awareness of belonging to Christ, and so of having an ideal that is as large as the world, begins to fade. Man's true desire is to build something great, something that remains, something that leaves a mark in the history of the world. Nothing is more opposed to the human stature to which Christ has called us than a narrow heart, than having a petty aim at the outset, than trying to secure oneself against life's storms. The decisive step in every education, then, is the enlargement

---

[49]   St. Thomas Aquinas, *Summa Contra Gentiles*, III, 127,7.

of the measure one's own heart. This is also essential for the beauty of anything that one builds: a man who is not prepared to invest a lot in what he does is an "ugly" man, and what he does is ugly, because it is the mirror of his meanness. For the same reason, being poor is not neglecting propriety in dress or the cleanliness of one's rooms. In sum, if you want to live out this great experience of building yourself and the world that we call poverty, you have to keep alive the enthusiasm of your belonging to Christ in the Church.

A second methodological observation to keep in mind is that you start putting poverty concretely into action by voluntarily sacrificing some particular possession. Otherwise, education will never happen. One is educated to a principle only by doing, that is, by beginning to live the principle out in at least one detail, so as to be able to live it out in everything. How do we educate ourselves to reach the stature of the man who uses everything without being enslaved by anything? By beginning, in at least one particular, to make the availability of my goods a living reality.

We are dealing here with a twofold pedagogical principle having two faces. The first is that if you want to get educated you have to commit yourself to doing something. The second is that this doing is an exemplification, an introduction to the whole by way of a particular. How can I educate a person's life to gratuity? I start by asking him to live 15 minutes of gratuity during the week. How can I educate a person to life as a prayer? I start by asking him to pray. How, then, can I educate a person to stop feeling that what he has is his property? When a mother thinks about herself and about her time, energy, and money, if she is a healthy person, she feels that they are all a function of her family. Feeling this way has become almost an "instinct" in her by dint of the exercise of her responsibility as a mother. Which is just the point: you become educated, not by cutting off all at once some particular possession, but by living it in terms of its relation to your task. And this also means keeping it small, like a mother who, for the good of her children, can't afford to buy everything that she would like.

There is, finally, a third aspect. Where is it that we are educated to the beauty, to what I have called the "luminousness," of poverty? Education to poverty occurs in one's relationship with the authority set over the vocational company in which Christ has placed us. One's constant, willingly embraced, intelligent, free relationship with authority, with one's superiors, is the greatest help in following this path to the end. This relationship is the context in which one is educated to a constant effort to change and to a responsibility for everything, because everything is a sign of Christ. This relationship is therefore a responsibility that is at once cheerful and serious: cheerful, because it is not a nightmare, but serious because it means that we have to be at work, a constructive work of verifying the purpose for which we use what we use and for which we have what we have.

This assumption of personal responsibility is more important and decisive than any rule. Fixing rules can lead to the diminishment of one's responsibility, which is the exact opposite of education.

IV
Virginity

The Apex of the Human

Obedience, poverty, and virginity mutually imply one another. They are, in fact, dimensions of the new man as such. That having been said, virginity is the word that of the three best sums this novelty up, because it synthesizes man's true attitude towards himself, towards others, and towards things.

Virginity is not something that we must first acquire or that we are called to attain in the future. Virginity has been given to us through the grace of Baptism, even if we do not realize it. We often live forgetful of this. There is thus no more valuable work than that of regaining awareness of our face[50]. Especially since the time of the French Revolution, the Christian people has felt virginity to be a segment of Christian life, a way of living reserved to certain persons only. In some cases, this feeling has been accompanied by a sense of pity, of the sort that one has for the "condemned." It is not difficult to come up with examples of this marginal status of virginity in the under-

---

[50] The following reflections take their origin from meditation on a few of texts of Luigi Giussani that I consider to be particularly valuable. See Luigi Giussani, *Il tempo e il tempio* (Milan: BUR, 1995), 11-35; *Si può vivere così?*, 349-369; *Alla ricerca del volto umano* (Milan: BUR, 1995), 83-92; *L'attrativa Gesù*, 50-52, 117f.

standing of the Christian people. Even when virginity was exalted, it was still regarded as something reserved for the few. The result was that virginity, whether it was regarded with distant reverence or with commiseration, was not perceived as something belonging essentially to man's concrete life.

Fr. Giussani has taught me to look at virginity from a completely different point of view. In my opinion, one of his greatest merits is precisely that he has taken virginity from the world's sidelines and put it back at the world's heart, thus restoring it to what was really its rightful place all along. Virginity is not in the first instance a way of life set apart for a few, but the deepest form of Christian life as such. To be sure, it becomes a specific form of life for some, but this is only so that everyone can experience it. Even we may entertain the limited view of virginity which I was referring to above, since practically everyone around us takes it for granted. We, too, therefore need a change of mentality, which consists in moving from the conception of virginity as an experience that is very grand, but reserved for the few, to a conception of virginity as the truth of the world. Virginity has to do with this life, even though its roots lie in a deeper level of reality.

Only if we enter into this way of looking at things can we realize in a vital manner that virginity does not originate from renunciation. All are called to virginity, and priests, who in addition are called to live it out as a form of life, are a prophecy of what the whole world is destined for. This change of perspective in thinking about virginity entails a change of perspective in understanding the vocation of the priest itself. Virginity is a part of the prophetic task to which the priest is called, precisely because virginity is the beginning of true humanity.

The Roots of Virginity

What is the source from which the new man is born? Baptism. Virginity is rooted in Baptism, which, grafting us onto the life of Christ, makes us partakers in his way of perceiving, seeing, understanding, and affectively possessing everything. Baptism shapes the life of the Christian in accord with the attitude that Christ had towards himself, towards persons, and towards things.

Virginity, then, is nothing other than imitation of Christ, an identification with his humanity worked by Baptism in our lives: an imitation of the way of life of a man who was God, a progressive identification with the life of Jesus, a progressive discovery of what Baptism has made us. In Baptism all are given a potentiality that requires development: we know, in fact, that every seed that is not cultivated sooner or later rots.

The gift of virginity is therefore born of faith. There is no other way of understanding or explaining it. The fact that this gift is so little understood and appreciated is due to the immaturity of people's faith, because virginity is incompatible with a solely natural vision of life. If, in fact, the flowering of virginity as the unfolding of Baptism occurs in a specific form of life, we can understand it only when we look at life with the eyes that we receive from Baptism, that is, in faith. In the same way, the immaturity of our experience of virginity is closely connected with the immaturity of our experience of faith, that is, of how we look at the world and ourselves, and with the immaturity of our experience of belonging to Christ. Virginity is a flower that is not born spontaneously, but that blooms and blooms again only as a consequence of the discovery that following Christ is the greatest good for men. If you do not live the experience that

Christ is the creator and Lord of life, the giver of every good, and the guide of existence, how can the experience of virginity flower anew in you? Every contradiction will become a reason for doubt and difficulty.

A *Vertiginous Experience*

If virginity is the imitation of Christ, what is the focal point of this imitation? The Gospels attest clearly to the fact that Jesus' life consists in being the one sent by the Father, in being totally relative to him, completely determined by obedience to him. By the same token, his way of entering into relation with people and things was shaped by acknowledgment of the place that the Father had assigned them[51].

Here we catch sight of the dizzying height on which virginity is perched: by identifying us while still on earth with the life of Jesus, it makes us enter into the mystery of the Trinity, into the divine gaze, into the heart of God. It introduces us, while still in time, into something eternal. It gives to every moment of our lives, to all of our relationships, a mysterious but real incorruptibility, and it imbues us with the certainty that time will not sweep them away. This certainty is the origin of the splendor that people saw in the gaze, in the words, and in the actions of Jesus. Virginity is participation in the mentality, in the heart, and in the gaze of Christ. The letters of St. Paul, especially the ones he addresses to the communities he holds particularly dear, abound with references to this fact: "have in you the same mind that was in Christ Jesus" (Phil 2:5); "we have the mind

---

[51] See Luigi Giussani, Si *può vivere così?*, 118f, 350f; Si *può (veramente?!) vivere così?*, 520.

of Christ" (1 Cor 2:16). Virginity is an identification with how Christ thought, with how Christ looked at things. We should contemplate again and again the gaze with which Jesus looked upon Zacchaeus, upon the Samaritan Woman, upon the widow of Nain, upon the lilies of the field, upon the birds of the air: a gaze that he draws from prayer, from his unbroken relationship with the Father[52]. In this way we also understand that virginity is the work of the Holy Spirit in us: "he will guide you into all truth. . . . He will glorify me, because he will take from what is mine and he will announce it to you" (Jn 16:13-15). Identification with Jesus' gaze is the work of the Holy Spirit and our life.

At this point we glimpse the profound bond uniting virginity, poverty, and obedience. Without the experience of virginity as a matter of communion in our relationships, there can be no poverty. On the other hand, if you cannot live obedience, you cannot understand poverty. Poverty, in the same way as virginity, is a measure that is being given to me continuously: it is not something that I have learned once and for all and that I now simply apply, and obedience is precisely acceptance of the fact that the measure of my life is given to me by another, moment by moment.

Sacrifice

In the process of becoming conformed to the thought, the feelings, and the affectivity of Jesus, one cannot avoid the path that he himself trod to the end: the fulfillment of our

---

[52] See, for example, Luigi Giussani, Si può vivere così?, 75f, 277; Si può (veramente?!) vivere così?, 158, 160, 207f, 364, 382, 507; Vivendo nella carne (Milan: BUR, 1998), 187f.

humanity in virginity must pass through death in order to attain the resurrection. There has to be sacrifice.

Why is this? I would like to begin by inviting reflection on a fact: sacrifice is a given that is massively present in our lives. We have to recognize that life calls for sacrifice, that sacrifice is a condition of life. This does not mean that accepting it is an easy and straightforward thing to do. One of the things that has most struck me in my experience as a priest is that, when people complain of being hit by the sacrifices that life demands, they never tire of asking the reason why: why separations, why injustices, why the supreme contradiction of death?

The priest is powerless to help people facing these questions if he does not carry them himself like an open wound. I can say that, over the years, I have become more and more clearly aware of the following answer: sacrifice has its origin in the particular condition in which we happen to live within time. We find ourselves, in fact, half way between the ephemeral possession of the world that we are leaving behind and the full possession of the truth that we have not yet reached. It sometimes seems to us that we are leaving behind something that we have, while we are not yet able fully to obtain what we do not have. St. John says in his first letter: "we do not yet know what we will be" (see 1 Jn 3:2). In this space between certainty and the "fascination of nothingness"—as the Bible calls it (see Wis 4:12)—the devil insinuates his trickery. The father of lies centers all of his efforts on making us think that the all is nothing and that nothingness is all. This is why the judgment of faith is so important. There are times when only the memory of the encounter with Christ can shake us and make us realize that we are "drowning in a glass of water."

Fr. Giussani has a name for this passage from appearance to truth: "detachment"[53]. Detachment from what? From an instinct-ruled possession, even as we already experience in this detachment the dawn of a new kind of possession. In this detachment, we have the experience of the hundredfold already on earth that Jesus promised us (see Mk 10:28-30)[54].

Without this detachment, we do not have more, we only think we do. The truth is that what we hold in our hands is used up and destroyed. The only way to save things, others, and oneself is to accept a distance, that is to say, to acknowledge the otherness of what we love, to recognize that the authentic and total point of reference for the other can never be me, but only the mystery of God. Instinctuality leads us to identify the Thou with the I, to want the I to be God for the Thou. This is the path towards the destruction of the other and of oneself. Romantic aesthetics understood this well. Indeed, it made it the center of its thought and inspiration, identifying love with death. Love is death because in love—understood as a matter of instinct without distance—the other can only be sacrificed to the I.

Election

God—the God of Abraham, of Isaac, and of Jacob—has a method for communicating himself to human beings and for getting what most interests him through their thick

---

[53] See, for example, Luigi Giussani, Si *può vivere così?*, 351ff.

[54] Fr. Giussani paraphrases this passage of the Gospel thus: "you will possess a hundred times as much, albeit at the price of a sacrifice." See Luigi Giussani, *Vivendo nella carne*, 187.

skulls: the choice of some as points from which to radiate out to the others to whom he wants to give life. This is absolutely clear throughout God's whole history with human beings beginning with Abraham. God chooses one in order to gather the others around him. This is true both in the dimension of the individual person and in the dimension of the people. God has chosen one man in order to create a people, and he has chosen one people in order to gather together the other peoples. The word that describes this divine dynamic and method is "election" (from the Latin *eligo*, I choose).

Now, if this method that God uses in relation to man is so decisively important, it cannot help but have something to do with virginity as well. And as a matter of fact, the reason that God has chosen some is so that all might be enabled to live what I have described. God has chosen some so that all might be able to realize that they can have this experience in their own lives. How has he chosen them? He has sent his Son, he has chosen his Son, who in turn has chosen others who have begun to live with him in this way. And these others, in their turn, have been transmitters of election all the way down to us.

What is the ultimate significance of the life that Christ has brought, of the gaze with which he regarded things and persons, of the perception that he had of beings, of the world, of others, of history? It is the awareness that everything is connected with the mystery of the Father. Christ came and died on the Cross in order to introduce us into the experience of his relationship with the Father, in order to bear witness to the truth of the Father. Therefore, insofar as virginity is a new way of relating to oneself and to others, its origin, meaning, and form lies in Christ, in the mystery of his person. Consequently, an essential feature of virginity is its character as testimony, as "martyrdom," to use the ancient terminology[55]. From this point of view, the experience of virginity is the same thing as passion for the glory of Christ: the passion that Christ, the one who has made my life true, may be known by others too and so transform their lives as well, so that the world be more human. Virginity is a way of life that cries out the name of Christ, that cries out that Christ is the only reason to live and the only chance for fullness of life. Virginity is a prophecy because those who live it shout out loud and clear to the world that the truth of the world is Christ, that Christ is everything, that Christ is the meaning of everything[56].

But I would like to add an important remark. God—I have said—is so moved by his personal love for every human being that He calls some to virginity. Virginity, then, is born as an answer to a predilection and, as such, is a relationship, not a negation of relationships. Virginity is love, the apex of love, because it is nothing other then the response to the predilection of Christ within which one then learns truly to love everything else. Only if one experiences this fact can one live out the sacrifice that virginity requires: one can live out sacrifice only if it is an offering to *someone.*

Preference

Election has to do with preference. God's method is very individual, because not only does he choose one people in

---

[55]   See Luigi Giussani, Si *può vivere così*?, 350.

[56]   See Luigi Giussani, Il *tempo e il tempio*, 21ff.

order to reach all, but even within this one people he maintains different relationships with each member. We can glean a truth about the deep structure of reality from consideration of this divine method: everything not only receives its being, but also a particular relationship of its own with the *Logos*, and is, for this reason, a particular expression of the *Logos*. This is true of everything that exists, but it emerges with the utmost clarity in man, who is the apex of creation. Every single human being is a particular expression of the *Logos*. Each man has a different form of relating to the *Logos*, and this is precisely what the human spirit is. What I have called "preference," then, is built into the structure of being, a structure that will continue to exist even beyond time as well.

God has put the stamp of preference on us men who are made in his image. For us, after all, to live is to *prefer*. Life is made up of proximities and distances. I feel that one person is more important for me than another, I feel that one book is more interesting than another, I am struck by one piece of music while another leaves me cold. The same dynamic shows up in our intellectual knowledge: knowing is ordered according to one's point of view. In sum, preference is a sort of realization of the particular proximity or distance that persons or things have in our regard, of the different importance that they have for us, of the different attraction that they exercise on us, and, finally, of the different role that they play in our relationship with the Mystery. And it should be noted that preference is a peculiar characteristic of man's affective life. On the other levels of nature, what might look like preference is really nothing but mechanical reaction.

God loves man, and so has chosen that man's relationship with other men should echo the life God himself lives with man. He has not merely given a commandment, but has placed within man the experience of desire, of attraction, and of relish, an experience that he intends as the portal through which man comes little by little to understand the infinite horizon that God has destined for him.

Preference is a school; it is a way in which God teaches us himself through particular proximities. The principal aim of preference, therefore, is openness to being, not closure to it. The goal of preference is to teach us the value of everything through a particular example that is affectively interesting for us. It is a method, because, if I were equally interested in everything, I would end up adhering to nothing; if all persons had the same significance for me, I would be equally distant from all of them, and I would end up not getting involved with any of them. I would try to get involved with all of them, and I would be overwhelmed. Preference is thus the method by which the Lord continually renews the freshness of our gaze upon the world[57]. Preference is therefore not an invitation to exclusion, but a form of education.

Preference is a school for understanding the Mystery on which we depend, a school that opens us to God and to others. In saying this, I have already highlighted the risk inherent in this method that God has chosen: the risk that our lived experience of it that will be nothing more than a feeling of dogged attachment to some particular. The first and fundamental preference that God gives in life is our mother. Without this preference, our personality collapses, as the sciences of pedagogy and psychology have amply demonstrated. If you take away a child's mother in its first

---

[57] See Luigi Giussani, *"Tu" (o dell'amicizia)* (Milan: BUR, 1997), 98.

years, it loses the primary relationship that maintains it in being. But if this preference does not mature over time, if it does not evolve (and this evolution may also involve pain) on a path of openness to being, to others (and the role of the father is fundamental here), it can become the tomb of the person. This is true of every preference.

Preference, then, must not be erased or overcome, as if it were a bad one-sidedness, but lived out in accord with the reason for which it is given. This is clearly the case in friendship, which can either enhance everything that is true and good in us, but when it becomes a self-enclosed clique, a private club where the windows are never opened, it can also weigh my person down.

Preference has the unique power to give us a new birth, to reawaken in us the taste for being: when a friendship is born, when one falls in love, when one feels truly loved and appreciated, then one is reborn, one rediscovers one's usefulness in the world. But, precisely if it is going to perform this function, it has to be lived out as a form of obedience[58]. Preference is a gratuitous event that is neither predicted nor planned. You don't plan to fall in love, you can't plan a friendship, a love, a relationship. You discover it, you find it as a given. Preference is obedience because it is a gift, a sign of God in one's life. It is obedience to God and to reality; if its true purpose is not understood, it turns against us and kills us. At this point, the need for sacrifice in order for our relationships to be true comes once more to the fore. If one has a possessive relationship with the person that one prefers, one clasps him so tightly to oneself that one suffocates, that is, destroys him. This is the temptation of mothers with their children,

---

[58] See, ibid., 100-102.

of men with women, of women with men, and of friends with their fellows.

Preference for Christ

At bottom, the entire existential question posed by the phenomenon of preference that we discover at work in us is summed up and clarified in faith, where it takes the form of a necessary predilection for Christ. It is only by living out preference for Christ that we can learn to live every other preference in a true way. A preference becomes true only if it is a school of preference for Christ, if what is sought in it is preference for him. The question that each one of us has to ask himself in living out a preference is this: what am I seeking in this relationship that is so dear to me? If one asks oneself this question sincerely, the preference becomes a school.

A priest friend of mine once asked me: "how do you keep your life focused so that everything is defined by your vocation and not by your worry about what you may say or do?" I answered as follows: seek out those faces who helped you do that and you'll get from them a light that you can radiate in turn onto the faces of others.

In reading Thomas Aquinas' *Questions on Charity*, I was very struck by his tendency to identify love and preference. Love is always a preferential love. There is no other way for me concretely to embrace everything except through preference. God did not become "man," but "that man": Jesus of Nazareth. This was the condition of his being able to embrace everyone. Through his encounter with the Samaritan, with Zacchaeus, through that small handful of people, he met with the whole world.

Our greatest gratitude as Christians springs from the fact that God has given us a home. He has not left us alone in the night, in the cold, to fight it out against everything and everyone, but he has given us a home as a starting-point. The Council says that the Church is a pilgrim in the world[59]: this means that the Church is missionary. We are pilgrims because the home that has been granted to us is an anticipation of our definitive home, but is not yet that definitive home. God has made us a home where we can be continually regenerated for mission, in order to go out, call others, and be a sign of memory in the world's great forgetfulness.

Virginity Towards Oneself

I would like to conclude by suggesting a few ideas about virginity as a virtue in relation to oneself. For virginity has to do with how we look at ourselves, at our past, present, and future.

In order to grow up, the first thing we need to do is to work out a balanced relationship with our own past. For example, it is important to come to an authentic judgment about the place that our parents have in our lives. Otherwise, we are left with just two options: either the sentimental attitude of those who cannot detach themselves from their parents, or the censorship of those who want to burn their bridges with bad experiences from their earlier lives. This is also true generally. But it is unthinkable that your present and future life can be true unless you are reconciled with the whole of your past.

---

[59] See *Lumen Gentium*, 8 and 48-50.

So virginity towards oneself means first of all to love oneself as one is, to accept one's own limits, one's own defects, one's own sins. Not in order to approve of them, but because acceptance of one's own evil is the condition of change. It is the beginning of freedom and of spiritual, mental, and even physical health. Virginity is freedom from oneself, and the most striking aspect of this freedom has to be self-acceptance. The high-point of self-acceptance is in turn acceptance of one's own limitedness, of one's own fragility, and of one's own sin.

This virginity as freedom from oneself expresses itself most completely when one becomes a function of the work of Christ and gives oneself for the glory of Christ. Freedom from oneself is gift of self. As we have seen, the essence of the priestly life consists in this. Freedom from oneself is a gift of oneself to Christ who is present: to proclaim Christ present, to make him present in the sacraments, to educate people: all this is a gift of self aimed at making Christ known and loved.

Virginity in relation to oneself is, in the second place, the ability to be independent of others' judgment. We lose so much time and so much peace because we depend too much on other people's judgment. The point is not that we should be indifferent to the judgment of others, but that we should be attentive to the true judgment of those who are passionate about our lives, who know and love us, instead of to everything that others say about us. The stature of our existence is defined by Christ.

In this sense, virginity towards ourselves also has to do with how we live out the responsibilities that are entrusted to us. This is also a crucial point for priests. If we are are given responsibility, we need to accept it and live it out because it is given to us. If, however, it is not given to us, let's not worry about it because then we will have less to answer for before God.

I once asked a fencer, Mauro Numa—who had spent his entire life from the age of eight training 10 hours a day, including Christmas, Easter, and Sundays—to tell me what the hardest moment of his life had been. He answered: "the hardest moment hasn't come yet, and it will be when I have to leave the piste." I asked him to explain why. "Because the hardest thing for a man is to leave the piste where he fights." For our part, we need have no fear of being asked to leave the piste. Our dignity, like our responsibility, is not diminished because a role or a charge is taken away from us.

Another aspect of this ability to be independent of the judgment of others has to do with our work. If you cannot live out your work commitments with detachment and balance, then clearly your affective equilibrium is still immature. We are often driven by the need to feel confirmed by the success of the work that we do; the pursuit of this success compels us to sacrifice silence, prayer, and our relations with our truest friends. The person constantly surrenders to everything that he is asked to do at work for fear of disappointing the expectations of those to whom he has to report. The issue here is not just voluntarism. It is much more serious than that because its roots lie in the inability to focus one's affectivity on the event of Christ. The Bible speaks of an enemy who " prowls around like a roaring lion seeking someone to devour" (1 Pt 5:8): this roaring lion is often our own heart in search of something other than Christ as an object on which to pour out our affective energies.

Both in the case of my role and in the case of my work, I run the great risk of being happy, not because of the special love that I receive from Christ, but because I do certain things or live in environments where I get superficial affective compensation. All of that brings about considerable psychophysical wear and tear, because one is always bent on chasing after something that is outside of oneself and one is never happy with what one has already received.

V
Sexuality

The Earthly and the Divine Meet

I would like to fill out the observations that I have made about virginity with a few remarks on sexuality. My aim is not to work out a systematic reflection. My only concern is to suggest what I consider to be the main guidelines for educating young people called to virginity as a form of life for us to help them achieve a serene and mature relationship to their sexuality.

Sexuality is a great gift of God that constitutes the human person down to his roots and thus imparts its character to the most important dimensions of his being.

On account of the sexual difference and the physiological, biological, and psychological opening that it creates, the person is constituted first and foremost as relation to otherness. This means that we depend on others for our realization. But this also means that our joy consists in finding our fulfillment in relation with others. This brings us to the phenomenon of love, a word enriched with an infinity of nuances and meanings, precisely because it involves an infinite series of experiences, all of them important for man's life. Seen in this first perspective, which we could call the perspective of dependence, sexuality opens before us the deep mystery of human life, its origin, and its destiny. For the fact that we need others shows clearly the structural insufficiency of our being as humans, but it also means that our happiness lies in the fulfillment that others achieve with us.

The other essential dimension of the human person revealed by sexuality is fruitfulness. The love between the man and the woman does not merely refer to the presence of the other or others, to children, but also opens up prospects for relation that will never close again. Sexuality underscores that man and woman are placed in the world as a need for relation and as a capacity to generate. Sexuality expresses their openness to the history of the world and the connection between each human being and all his fellows.

Now, precisely because it involves man's fundamental experiences, sexuality influences every aspect of the life of the person, from his animal instincts to his highest capacity for cognition, intellection, and free planning. Jean Guitton, whose philosophical thinking is saturated by the theme of the encounter between time and the eternal, has written that no event of man's life matches sexuality as a meeting place of heaven and earth, dust and sublimity:

> There is no function of the psyche, there is no sensation or image, with which the sexual instinct cannot associate itself, even without the subject's awareness, and perhaps even more so when the subject is not fully conscious of it. The sexual instinct can derail the noblest sentiments and make the purest sight ambiguous. But its fire can also nourish the highest activities, it can awaken the gift of self, it can promote artistic creation. And one can say that, even when it is contained or inhibited, it is nonetheless always at work, because it gets transferred to every analogical object[60].

---

[60] Jean Guitton, *L'amore umano* (Milan: Rusconi, 1989), 164.

It is just this complexity of the phenomenon of sexuality that accounts for the constant and common temptation to isolate one or the other of its aspects. One of the most blatant contemporary forms of this division, apart from the pathological species known as pornography, is the one that severs the aspects of sexual attraction and sexual generation, the pleasure that sexuality brings and the responsibility connected to it. On the opposite side—but the opposition is only apparent, because the underlying mentality is the same—there is a tendency to seek a fruitfulness severed from the sexual union between man and woman.

By means of its composite and complex nature, sexuality actually teaches us the opposite lesson: the sublime can be perceived and encountered only in the earthly. By the same token, it is in Christianity that sexuality can be understood in all its greatness: for Christianity is the proclamation that God has mixed himself up with space and time, that he has become man, that, except for sin, he has taken on our humanity completely, down to its most hidden recesses.

The carnal dimension of the encounter between man and woman always contains the spiritual dimension. In spite of that, it is often experienced as an occasion for furtive episodes. This leaves plenty of room for gross distortion. Attraction to another person, originally called to become a sign of the Mystery in one's life, can be distorted into an urge to exploit for base ends.

The only way, then, to live out sexuality with respect for oneself and for the other is in terms of a balanced conception of the human: human beings are neither beasts nor angels, but they partake of both natures. The idea of man that has prevailed in the modern period is characterized by a profound dissociation between matter and spirit. This dissociation has been given a theoretical justification by philosophers such as Descartes and Spinoza, for whom man is on the one side a sort of machine (*res extensa*) and on the other side a sort of angel (*res cogitans*). Human relationships are accordingly in certain respects relationships among things and in other respects relationships among pure spirits. The opposite is true. Man is not the union of two juxtaposed things, but the inseparable unity of his bodily and spiritual dimensions. If we do not acknowledge this, we cannot give a justification of the importance of the work of education. Indeed, the most consistent thing would be to deny that education is even possible. For the task of education consists precisely in enabling the person to discover the eternal within time.

A Gift to be Lived Out Responsibly

Here is another observation from Guitton:

> Of course, spirit dreams of an experience in which the ardor of the senses and mystical renunciation fuse into one. This is the illusion of false mystics. . . . On the other hand, it is the privilege only of the true mystics to experience, at times without any artificial effort, certain states in which a total sacrifice of self is linked with an extraordinary happiness. In the normal and common run of things, unfortunately, agape and eros diverge and charity is born of renunciation, whereas the joy of the senses almost always presupposes an impoverishment of love[61].

---

[61] Ibid., 192.

There isn't anyone who doesn't want to be able to live out the greatest sensual experience while having the greatest spiritual experience, but this is, except in totally exceptional cases, an abstract utopia. The normal state of affairs is characterized instead by the need to accept a certain mortification of the erotic aspect of sexuality in the name of a truer love.

In order to live out sexuality authentically, we need an education, and, as Aristotle teaches, education is a matter of avoiding opposite excesses[62].

One possible excess is to think that sexuality is an untamable demon, and that human beings are objects possessed by it. The opposite excess is to think that for some, for example, for those who have chosen to dedicate themselves to God in virginity, sexuality doesn't exist. These are both mistaken beliefs that negate and exclude what is in fact the only viable path: the path of education, which happens when we seriously and serenely entrust ourselves to those who have the task of helping us and guiding us towards the maturity of our vocation.

There are two characteristics of this work of education that I would like to highlight above all. The first is the need for humor. The devil likes to make us believe there we are the most extraordinary sinners the world has ever seen. Humor is the ability to look at our limits reasonably, encouraged by faith in the One who, having created us together with other persons, and having given us sexuality as one of the distinguishing marks of our being, will guide us and will also have mercy on our sins. This irony enables us to stay on the path towards the concrete ideal that Christ has revealed for our life without getting discour-

---

[62] See Aristotle, *Nicomachean Ethics*, 1106B.

aged. This is the only way to prevent the sense of our falli-
bility from obscuring the fascination of what Christ has
given to our life.

The second aspect is the need for sacrifice. We mustn't
think that we can do anything we want, and the weight of
the acts that we have committed makes itself felt longer
and more strongly in this area than in others. In this sense,
the purification of the imagination has to be a permanent
dimension of our education. For sexuality floods and infus-
es our imagination with a continual offering of images and
subjects. Guitton goes so far as to speak of "a sort of hal-
lucinatory need, which is much harder to conquer, because
it is based on the imagination within." He then observes
that "the fear of a danger is much more difficult to bear
than the danger itself, and one can fight against the pricks
of sensation, but it is hard to resist the bedazzlement of
the imagination"[63]. Imagination is much more powerful in
the domain of sexuality than it is in others. The main thing,
then, is not to make an effort to avoid falling, but to keep
one's eyes on the educational path which one is part of and
truly to love it, to love it so much that one loves the sacrifice that it requires. A single sin does not amount to a radical error; radical error is a tendency, a tendency to evil. To
forbid certain acts does no good if the only thing animat-
ing it is a spirit of duty: that just makes you desire all the
more. What counts is cultivating and nourishing day in and
day out the sense for the commanding presence of the
ideal in our lives.

Sexuality is such a great good that it reveals to us the
face of man and the face of God at one and the same time.
But it is a good that it is hard to live out, which is why God

---

[63] Jean Guitton, *L'amore umano*, 165.

is merciful. God— Karl Barth rightly said—is always different from every possible imagination, and therefore breaks and splits open the petrified shells in which egoism never ceases trying to encase love[64]. The most important thing is that one's life be handed over to God; no one can claim to be wise enough to walk the path by his own power. We do not have to be not perfect men, but holy men, that is, men handed over to Christ. The handing over of oneself, which happens when one opens oneself sincerely to one's superiors, is like a fire that purifies the nugget of gold from its earthy dross. What we should fear most is mediocrity: that is, that something might remain unburned in this purifying fire. Happiness is a continual conquest, which our self-love continually endangers.

Relating to the Opposite Sex

Education to a peaceable relationship with one's sexuality must also firmly establish in the person desiring to live in virginity an ability to relate serenely with the opposite sex. Demonizing or fleeing from relationships with the opposite sex would be as one-sided as the obliviousness of someone who refuses to see how these relationships can be problematic. You cannot educate by hiding problems, but only by helping to face them.

When I speak to the young men whom I guide and accompany on the way to the priesthood, I often stress that the female presence is very important in a man's life. The life of Jesus himself shows us this. There is no religious

---

[64] See Karl Barth, *Introduzione alla teologia evangelica* (Milan: Bompiani, 1968), 14.

experience that has valorized the presence of the woman as much as Christianity. Consider the fact that Jesus, God, was born of a woman; the first proclamation of the Resurrection was communicated to a woman; Jesus set apart a special place for women in his life. He exalted their dignity and the significance of their presence in his community, which was a revolutionary way of acting for that time, from the historical-social point of view.

More than any other Pope, John Paul II has underscored the extremely high regard in which the Church holds women. Two of his encyclicals have focused on this very topic from different points of view: *Mulieris Dignitatem* and *Redemptoris Mater*. Balthasar has brought out the decisive importance of the female figure in the Church alongside that of the man as an icon of the Church's maternal, and not merely institutional, character and of the relationship between these two aspects[65]. More generally, recent theology has emphasized topics that had previously been left in the background, for example, the spousal relationship between Christ and the Church, or between the priest and the Church.

The experience of generation disposes the woman to play within the life of the family and of society a fundamental role as a witness to the capacity for disinterested welcoming and giving. The woman, moreover, is usually attentive to the signs given by the other for her, which, often because of superficiality, as well as sometimes because of vulgarity, the man is incapable of imagining.

My point here has been to recall just a few aspects of the way in which the Christian experience leads one to look

---

[65] See Hans Urs von Balthasar, *Sponsa Verbi*, 153-162; *Lo Spirito e l'istituzione*, 158-162.

on woman with admiration. Each one of us is called to enter more and more consciously into this gaze.

To be sure, every person has his own sensibility, his own level of maturity. Every encounter that has taken place has a value, a space in each person's affectivity. In order to live out one's affectivity in an authentic way, one needs a purity that one never stops learning. One can always end up in situations of solitude, difficulty, and misunderstanding where it is easy to slip. This is true not only of the relationship between the sexes, but also of friendship and discipleship. For example, a person may become involved with us out of the need for consolation, comfort, and companionship; in cases like this, there is an increased risk of exploitation, and one has to be much more vigilant.

My own personal experience has taught me a general principle of which I am more and more convinced: the measure of the significance of your relationships with other people is the possibility of happiness, and you never build happiness by denying the past or by riding roughshod over others' good. We cannot help ourselves and others by mystifying the truth or killing charity: that always leads to even worse evils. Nevertheless, we can thank God that man can never make a mistake so bad that he could justifiably say "it's impossible to begin again."

There is a passage from Olivier Clément that can be read as a companion to my fragmentary considerations:

In 1956, freshly baptized and toiling to live out a life of humility and forgiveness, the context in which fidelity becomes possible, I had a conversation with a young Hungarian revolutionary about the enigmatic encounter between man and woman. "There is no mystery," he told me, "fidelity is a waste of time: it just ties you down." "But what do you feel whenever one of your more or less brief encounters is over?" He stopped for a moment to reflect, now that his aggression had subsided. "Sometimes," he said, "I feel like I've killed a bird." So the path is strewn with dead birds. . . . Today we have a functional, quantitative order of things, whose mechanism ignores the deep rhythms of life; it is opposed by the disorder of instinct, of unregulated sexual impulse. It seems that the only means we have left to get out of our abstraction and solitude is our body. Nevertheless, the charging and release of erotic tension only mimics the spiritual death that would be necessary in order to let the other be. Each partner is sent back to his solitary confinement. The thirst for the absolute leads us, consciously or no, to expect everything for an instant from a precarious being that itself would need to be saved; sooner or later we ignore, wound, destroy, Tristan or Don Giovanni. This transfers the search for the absolute to pleasure itself, the search for the sacred to profanation. So Narcissus sits again in front of his mirror; time blurs the mirror, so he needs to change it in order that he may be adored again, and, as everything gradually becomes profane, the profanation has to be heightened to transgression. "Liberation" finally leads to the acts of the butcher or of the slave. Georges Bataille celebrates the relation between victim and butcher [Marquis de Sade] as the supreme erotic relationship, perhaps even as ecstasy: if you do not know how to die so that the other can be, you make the other die in order to feel that you are[66].

---

[66] Olivier Clément, *L'altro sole* (Milan: Jaca Book, 1977), 46f.

Virginity and Fruitfulness

God's plan includes more than just physical fruitfulness, even though physical fruitfulness is the ordinary way for fecundity to happen. In the Hebrew tradition as it is expressed by the Old Testament, physical fruitfulness was identified with the blessing of God, and so the free choice of lifelong virginity was inconceivable. But Jesus brought into the world a different, or better, a more profound experience of fruitfulness: deeper because it is not a negation, not even a devaluation, of sexuality, but the orientation of it to a different goal, which consists in living it out like Jesus and for Jesus. He himself clarifies this concept in order to forestall every risk of egoism: "for some were born eunuchs from their mother's womb, others are made eunuchs by men, and others have made themselves eunuchs for the kingdom of heaven. He who has ears to hear, let him hear" (Mt 19: 12).

In this sense, virginity is the anticipation of man's life beyond time, where sexuality will still exist, but will be purified of concupiscence. Jesus states this clearly when he is asked by the Sadducees about the famous episode of the seven brothers: "they will neither marry nor be given in marriage" (see Mk 12:18-27). They will not marry, not because there will no longer be sexuality, but because it will no longer be dominated by concupiscence. The way sin-corrupted man lives out his desire is by reducing the other person to an instrument of his own satisfaction. In fruitful virginity, by contrast, this unitive energy is not denied, but is ordered towards a new goal: the creation and guidance of the people of God. Man's choice cannot bring this about; God chooses man, and man acknowledges this choice.

Glorification of the Senses

I would like to conclude these remarks with a statement that is bound to seem unacceptable to a certain puritanism: Christianity is the glorification of the senses. For Jesus says "blessed are the eyes that see what you see and the ears that hear what you hear" (see Lk 10:23-24). This glorification is the result of a journey involving the whole person— recall what was said about the liturgy—and a purification of the mind and heart.

God has made us human and he has saved us. Salvation has to do with man in his totality: the whole man is called to encounter Christ. We know God visibly, as a prayer of the Church puts it[67]. The purpose of the senses is the knowledge of Christ and of everything that leads to him. The knowledge of Christ is the fullness of the senses. It is essential that our relationship with him not be intellectualistic; otherwise our desire for affection will seek elsewhere. It has to be an experience of the entire person.

Our senses must therefore be educated. Reading, imagination, listening, the spoken word must be educated in order to become filled with Christ. Jesus says that it is impossible to serve two masters (see Lk 16:13). We cannot fill our eyes and ears with Christ and with what contradicts him. Each of us knows what is the biggest obstacle along the path of our own education. Especially when it comes to something as delicate as the education of our sexuality, we can never afford to lose sight of what life's happiness is. Only a clear judgment about that enables us to embrace the toil of the journey, the toil of asceticism.

---

[67] See the first Preface of Christmas.

VI
The Challenge of Fatherhood

A *Look at the Present Day*

I have said that the drama of human existence is relationship with the father. This has clearly been the case in every period of history, but it is especially so today.

The desire for privacy, for escape into one's past, the withdrawal into oneself, or into one's family home, and the disinterest in the *polis* that characterize many people's lives today derive from, among other things, a field experience of the father. When God first thought of the Church, that is, of a guided company, he thought of man's constitutive need for a father and a mother. He wanted us always to have fathers and mothers to accompany us.

The experience of the absence or abscondence of the father manifests itself in insecurity, lack of resolve, and resistance to being loved and guided. The experience of being loved and fostered by the mother is disproportionately important, even as the energy communicated through this relationship can find no outlets for creative self-expression. A fatherless young man is unable to take responsibility for his everyday choices, he feels that reality is hostile or is the arena of a challenge that costs too much psychic, spiritual, and effective energy. If you don't have a father, your life is populated with enemies.

More recently, especially since the 1970s, there has been a progressive attack on fatherhood. The stated goal of the revolutions of 1968 was precisely the destruction of the role of the father and of every authority. The figure of the father was frequently identified with that of the paternalistic master; analogously, the same period brought forth theories of the death of God. A certain one-sided feminism has further contributed to the depreciation of the father in his maleness. The result has been a general crisis of the family, centered on the separation between sexuality and generation, between sexuality and education: sex understood purely as play.

The daily news shows that the crisis now affects not just the experience of paternity and maternity, but the very possibility of giving these names a meaning. Think about heterologous insemination, which makes it impossible to know who one's father and mother are; think of appalling things like "renting" wombs or the cloning of human beings. Does being a father still have any meaning?

Everyone can understand that a "genetic" mutation has occurred, and is still occurring, in man's conception of himself and what a source of unhappiness and violence it is. The ultimate root of unhappiness and violence is precisely the absence of the experience of sonship. Sonship and paternity are strictly correlative. If one does not recognize that one is a son, if one does not recognize one's own father, one is unfruitful because one is incapable of penetrating into reality, of plowing the soil of the world. The experience of sonship, by contrast, turns into an ability to generate and to create; one is able to face reality, to express oneself, to communicate intense affections. Having gotten to know so many young men, I can say that even priestly vocation can be connected with the search for the father. No one should be scandalized by this: the experience of becoming a father in the priesthood can turn out to be a path to discovering a sonship that has been absent in one's life. The vocation can thus open itself to the search for the origin of oneself and to the recognition of what is other than oneself, of others, and of the Other.

Today's crisis of fatherhood goes hand-in-hand with the crisis of belonging, which is perhaps the acutest form of the crisis of contemporary Catholicism. The world has dismissed belonging as an expression of sectarianism, thus radically undermining faith's ability to be the form shaping the whole of life. The weakening of the experience of paternity makes the figure of God as father ethereal and thins out the affective and creative density of faith's presence in history.

God calls us to be fathers and mothers today. We cannot forget the present, the context in which this call is addressed to us, in which this possibility is offered to us.

What are we to do? In guiding the young men who come to me and whose superior I become when they join the Fraternity of St. Charles, the main thing I tend to emphasize is that there is no getting around one's own carnal father: the point is not to censor him, forget him, or neglect him, but accept him, love him, and perhaps rediscover him. One mustn't sublimate the fatherhood-sonship relations, censoring one's historically and carnally given father. One must rather rediscover it and relive it within a new relationship.

Young people need to be educated to live out in relation to themselves and to things (even before they live it out in relation to other persons!) the paternity that they have experienced in a weak or problematic way. This education demands of them acceptance of reality and of their own freedom. Acceptance of reality: my being is dependence and belonging because I did not originate myself; the fact that my birth lies some distance in the past does not cancel this dependence and belonging, but rather clarifies and deepens it. Acceptance of freedom: to live is to take up creatively the challenge of a task that has been assigned, a task that involves work, trials, and difficulties, but also rewards, joys, and gratifications, and a task that defines one's place in the history of men and of God with men.

What Sort of Fatherhood?

God is Father. Jesus Christ has revealed this definitive word about man and about history. God therefore places his seal on man by instituting in man a fatherhood similar to his own. How does God reveal his paternity to us? Through the paternity of human beings. If there are times when fathers disappoint, it is because, as Jesus says, "only one is Father" (Mt 23:9).

In chapters five and seven of the Gospel of St. John, we find a particularly suggestive expression of Christ's experience of his relationship with the Father. He gives voice to his feeling of being urgently called upon by the Father to work without rest: "My Father is always at work, and I, too, am always at work" (Jn 5:17). Fatherhood is tireless activity: its task is to welcome, preserve, correct, and foster growth. This is the task that Saint Joseph had with respect to Jesus: to protect him and bring him up[68].

Every father is an educator. To educate a person means to guide him to the knowledge of the path on which he is

---

[68] See Saint Bernardine of Siena, *Opera*, VII, 16, 27-30 (in *Liturgia delle Ore secondo il rito romano* [Vatican City: Libreria Editrice Vaticana, 1993], 1505f).

to realize the eternal plan for his life in time. An example of paternity that has always struck me occurs in Dante's *Inferno*. The poet meets a fellow-citizen who has been ill-treated and exiled as he was: Bruno Latini, a man of learning, a profound philosopher, and an authority on the stars. Dante regards him as the model of the man capable of guiding others to make their lives a sign of the divine in time; he therefore feels him to be a father. The poet then addresses him in the following words: "In my mind is fixed, and it warms my heart to recall / the dear paternal image / of you who led me step by step / to learn how man becomes immortal"[69]. Dante meets Brunetto among the sodomites, but, notwithstanding the moral judgment he makes on Brunetto, what concerns him is to throw into relief the place that Brunetto has had in his life. Brunetto was able to show him the path towards self-realization. Since Brunetto was an astrologer, Dante makes use of the metaphor of the star to indicate the sign of the eternal in time, by following which one cannot "fail to reach the glorious port"[70].

Dante thus seems to delineate a certain antinomy: on the one hand, the goal of education is to bring the person to autonomy, to the ability to face reality and to plan freely his own future; on the other hand, the person's maturity involves the awareness of his own ineliminable dependence. Aren't these two claims contradictory? For the contemporary mentality, they are: autonomy means not depending on another, but on oneself. Here we touch on what is the crucial question of the history of humanity and of each man's existence.

---

[69] *Inferno*, XV, 82-85.
[70] Ibid., 56.

The Christian experiences that he daily becomes more and more himself, with an identity of his own, by adhering to a Presence. As he journeys forward, he does not deny his own origin; on the contrary, he is born ever more profoundly from it—and just so becomes ever more profoundly himself.

Modern civilization has asserted from its very beginnings that the high-point of education is the severing of all bonds (think of Makarenko's *Pedagogy for Schools* or of Rousseau's *Emile*[71]). Let us instead go to a different source: the Mystery of the Trinity. The Son's absolute relativity or belonging to the Father was manifested in his cry of "my God, my God, why have you forsaken me?" (Mk 15:34), which is at one and the same time the moment of the greatest distance and the greatest proximity. The central chapters of John's Gospel show us Christ as the one sent by the Father. The Son has manifested himself in the full power of his mission for the whole of human history precisely through this absolute and free unity with the Father: "What I see him do, I always do," "What pleases him, I do" (cf. Jn 4:34; 5:19; 7:16; 8:28, etc.).

God's Spirit also evacuates the antinomy between freedom and belonging for us who thus share analogously in what Christ himself lived. He thereby enables us to experience that the greatest freedom lies in the greatest belonging. This experience is one that we live even before being able to describe it: nature itself plainly teaches that the constructive energy with which a person throws himself into history increases with his awareness of being loved.

---

[71] A. S. Makarenko, *Pedagogia scolastica sovietica* (Rome: Armando Editore, 1960); Jean-Jacques Rousseau, *Emilio*, in *Opere* (Florence: Sansoni, 1972).

The thought of God's fatherhood is always with me and is for me a source of continual wonderment, of a gratitude that is a matrix of rebirth for me. God has made me from nothing, because once I did not exist, and now I do. This experience is the beginning of freedom, for freedom is self-possession, full self-realization, and the first realization of oneself is the very fact of existing. Every fatherhood that would imitate God's is one that creates and accompanies, that calls forth, enhances, and preserves the freedom of the other. This is the raison d'être for the existence of the Church and every vocational company: to accompany our personal drama, so that the original perception of being loved may become a habitual awareness in us.

The other experience with which I identify God's fatherhood in my life is liberation from fear. St. Paul contrasts the slave and the son, and says: "all those who are guided by the Spirit of God are sons of God. And you have not received the spirit of slavery to lead you back in fear, but you have received a spirit of adoptive sonship through which we cry 'Father'" (Rom 8: 14-15). The slave's relation to the master is one of fear, because the master commands. The son's relationship with the father is one of freedom, because the father guides him. Because he belongs to the Father through the Spirit, the Christian recognizes that he is a son and experiences liberation from fear. St. Paul describes the Christian as a slave who has been set free and adopted as a son: "you are no longer a slave, but a freeman" (Gal 4:7). For St. Paul, liberation was his personal experience of passing from Hebraism to Christianity; for us it is emancipation from the laws of the world. The world has its laws, and whenever it speaks of liberation, what it is really talking about are new laws that beget new forms of slavery.

St. John has recorded for us these words of Jesus: "I no longer call you servants, but friends." These words set up a contrast between the servant and the friend that parallels the Pauline contrast between the slave and the son. Jesus goes on to explain "because I have told you everything" (see Jn 15:15). The servant lives in fear because he does not know: he knows only what he has to do from morning till evening, but he does not know the meaning that what he does has in the master's plan for his household. We, by contrast, are free because we know the truth (see Jn 8:32). We know that we have been saved at the cost of Christ's blood (see Rom 5: 6-10). This certainty removes fear from our lives. It takes away the fear that our limits and our sins are the final word about us. This is why Jesus identifies the essence of the Father with mercy.

What is it about us that keeps us prisoners? The past, when we do not believe that the Spirit of Christ is able to wipe away our evil; the present, when we imagine that our relationship with Christ is measured by our ability to respond, rather than by his continuous initiative in coming to us; the future, when we do not have enough faith to be able to hope.

"In love there is no fear" (1 Jn 4: 18). I am reminded of the Psalms and the Prophets that speak of God as a father who bends over his child, gathers him up, and holds him in his arms. "Even if your father and mother should abandon you, I will never abandon you" (see Ps 27:10; Is 49:15). The Prophets are given the task of tirelessly reminding Israel that God's fatherhood is inexorable, tender, and not at all generic. In Jesus' last hours (see Jn 12-17), he talks several times about the elimination of fear. On leaving the Apostles, Jesus gives them the Spirit, who will make Jesus' presence in their lives actual and concrete. Just as Jesus is the one on whom the Spirit descends and remains, the Christian is the one who in the Spirit experiences God permanently accompanying his life (see Jn 1:33; 3:34). The Spirit is like fresh and clear water that continually bubbles up from the depths of our being (see Jn 4:14) and enables us to recognize the outward and historical signs of Jesus' presence.

The Foundation of All Paternity

St. Paul states that God the Father is the source from which "every paternity is named in heaven and on earth" (Eph 3:15). When we talk about fatherhood, then, we are talking in the first instance about the mystery of the person of God the Father, of the one from whom all being takes its origin— "the source of being is in You," as a hymn from the liturgy of the hours has it[72]—and from whom each one of us, who at one time did not exist, but then began to exist, comes into being. This means that we have been wanted, loved by a Freedom, by a Person who has made us be and continues to do so. Our words prove inadequate to express the reality of the person of God the Father: they are a sort of stammer. We speak of this reality on the analogy of what we understand by "person." But, however imperfect the analogy is, it is true. The Father is a person: he is freedom, intelligence, will. He is a mysterious, infinite I who cannot be enclosed within our experiences of the I, and yet is a real I nonetheless.

He has made himself known. From all eternity, he has made himself known to the Son, and then, by a mystery

---

[72] See "Eterno Dio immutabile," hymn for mid-day prayer, in *Il libro delle ore* (Milan: Jaca Book, 1999), 61.

that is at the very center of the mystery that he himself is, he has willed something that would be above and beyond, and yet within, the dialogue between himself and the Son: he has willed us. He has expressed his paternity by willing us as sons who are like him and are capable of dialogue with him. He has willed us as his image, as the Bible puts it (Gen 1:26). Not only has he willed us into being, but he has accompanied us, and continues to accompany us, on the way to the destiny for which he has made us. He has not abandoned us to ourselves, to some unknown fate, but has instead made us for life.

How has the Father made himself known to us? By inaugurating a history that itself began with a father, Abraham, a man who allowed his life to be changed by following the voice in which the Father manifested himself. In doing so, he discovered that he was a father of infinite generations in the sight of the mysterious "Thou" who said to him "look at the heavens, count the stars; look at the sand on the seashore, count its grains: behold, your children will be even more numerous" (see Gen 13:16; 22:17). But Abraham felt God's fatherhood upon himself not only in imagining a distant future, but in perceiving the full force of the Presence that changed the way he looked at his wives, his children, his concubines, his animals. He began to take in the world with a gaze that had at last acquired unity, to see everything in function of the promise that he had received.

Abraham was the first human being to be defined entirely by the word spoken by Another. We do not know how Abraham was first reached by it, but this Word, this Presence did touch him and did begin to become flesh in him. The Word began to become flesh in him. Not, of course, in the full sense in which St. John says that the Word became flesh in Jesus of Nazareth (Jn 1:14), but in an initial, though real, form. In God, the word is initiative, action, and mobilizing presence: "Abraham, leave your country" (Jn 12:1), leave the certainties on which you have based your life until now, the the horizons in which you have been settled, because I am the only possible source of truth, the only possible source from which to build." To contemplate Abraham, this mysterious and incredibly great person, is to begin to understand something of ourselves.

What counts in life is faithfulness, the humility with which you follow the path along which God guides you. That was Abraham's greatness. He received the promise of innumerable children; God then gave him a son in his old age, when his wife was practically sterile (Gen 21:2). Abraham knew how to hope, he remained faithful to God, in the certainty that God would bring his work to completion. God is faithful, as St. Paul says (1 Cor 1:9), and faithfulness is the supreme form of imitating God.

A father is always the beginning of a people. This is true of Abraham. It is true of Christ, who, through the mystery of his death and Resurrection, immerses sonship vis-à-vis Abraham within his own Sonship and enables every human being to have an experience of sonship and fatherhood like his. This is how the Christian people is born. Our life has been gifted with an extraordinary, absolutely gratuitous and unexpected experience of being part of a people—not in a nominal sense, as if it were merely something written down on paper, but really—a people made up of particular faces, of dates, of events. A people defined by a clear belonging that is at the same time thrown wide open to the whole world.

As for priests, to speak of sonship and fatherhood is to speak of the fact that God has chosen them for a highly positive task. It is to speak of their desire to be responsible for the people that God has willed into being and that he entrusts to them.

Called to be Fathers in the Church

God's design comes to pass in history through a continual rebirth of his people, which is made possible by the presence of a "holy seed" (Is 6:13). This is still true of the Church today.

The world hates the Church, it perceives the Church as an intrusive and bothersome presence. Why? Because the Church recalls men to the truth, reminding them that no form of power can adequately answer their deepest needs. As T.S. Eliot once powerfully put it, the Church exists to remind man that lust, money, and power are incapable of quenching his heart's thirst[74]. This is not the only function of the Church, of course, but when human beings do not participate in its life and do not discover it as bearing a possibility of fullness, they see it merely as a source of intolerable claims, admonitions, and prohibitions.

Why is the Church important for man? It is the place of true paternity and maternity, which express the maturity and fullness of the human. Although paternity and maternity are physiologically and psychologically different, on a basic level they have the same value, because they share the same task of begetting and educating. They represent the highest form of participation in the end for which we exist.

---

[74] T.S. Eliot, Choruses from "The Rock", Collected Poems 1909-1962, Faber and Faber, 1963.

God is the one who begets and does not forsake, who admits to being and educates us in it. The first task of spiritual fatherhood is therefore to educate. Christ has left this task above all to holy Mother Church: she generates her children in the baptismal font, she feeds them, raises them, and sustains them through the sacraments, catechesis, and mutual belonging. Priests are the servants of the fatherhood of God and the motherhood of the Church.

I would like to allude to three aspects of the exercise of spiritual paternity that I consider to be essential. One of the constituents of the tradition of the Church is the liturgy. Consequently, a primary aspect of spiritual paternity is to make sure that this heritage is not lost, but rather imparts new life in today's different situations and encounters to those educated to receive it, to draw nourishment from it, and to taste its richness. We risk squandering this treasure when we reduce the liturgy to a dry repetition of formulas, either by treating it with lazy sloppiness or when—and this is only apparently the opposite—or celebrating it extravagantly and exaggeratedly.

A second decisive aspect of the exercise of spiritual fatherhood is the introduction to texts that over time become foundation stones on which to build a home. The suggestion of certain readings, accompanied by the explanation of why they should be read, is a privileged form of spiritual fatherhood.

A third aspect is education to community life, an education that can and should take place in the forms suited to this purpose. Trips, vacations, gatherings, moments of communion: all of these things can be effective ways of transmitting the value of, and the taste for, communion. By participating in these gestures of community, the person, almost without realizing it, is introduced into a form of life that will never leave him, even if it accompanies him only by a feeling of nostalgia. We educate to speaking, to listening, to "being together" in amusement, song, or silence: this is a new form of life that Christ in the Church brings to men through our friendship. It is a channel through which those who might feel the desire or the need for advice, an opinion, consolation, or a particular help will be able task for it.

An example that illustrates spiritual fatherhood is the relationship between St. Paul and the Corinthian Christians, children who were as beloved as they were unruly. Reading St. Paul's letters is always illuminating and comforting: in them we find his personality, his heart, and, at the same time, between the lines or sometimes explicitly stated, the events of his life, which is like a mirror of ours. Every Christian can compare his experience to Paul's.

There is a passage from the First Letter to the Corinthians that sets forth the substance of the paternity and maternity of the Apostle in relation to those entrusted to him. The community at Corinth was divided into factions that vied for supremacy, appealing now to one apostle, real or putative, now to another. Their faith became a reason for vainglory, as if it were not a gift of divine grace, but a merit of their own. St. Paul perceives this as a betrayal of his paternity, because he knows that paternity, maternity, and sonship are a pure gift. You become a father if you receive fatherhood from God the Father; you become a mother if you receive motherhood from the Church who is a mother. Paul does not hold back even from sarcasm, as long as he can get at and correct the deviations of the Corinthians: "you are full, you are rich, you are kings." You have started believing that you are masters of what has been given to you gratuitously; you have sought recognition as your own makers, and by doing that you look extremely ridiculous to us: "if at least you had become kings, then we could reign with you!" (1 Cor 4:8).

Paul shows what sort of difficulties the Apostle faces, that is, the father who is well aware that he has received something that he has to make fruitful through the gift of self. The sacrifice God asks can be total: foreshadowing the spectacles of the beasts and the massacre of Christians in the circus, Paul says that he has become "a spectacle to the world, to angels, and to men" (1 Cor 4:9). Confronted with the supposed wisdom of the Corinthians, he puts at the center the necessity of self-renunciation and self-gift as the condition for being a true father.

By means of the antinomies that he uses so masterfully, Paul explains who a father is: one whose sole interest is the gratuity of his act of begetting. For this reason, "even if we are insulted; we bless, even if we are persecuted, we bear it; even if we are calumnied, we console" (1 Cor 4:12-13), because we find our glory in what we have received and in what we can give (1 Cor 4:7). The Apostle concludes: "I write you these things because you are my beloved children. You may have ten thousand pedagogues, but not many fathers" (1 Cor 4:14-15). The pedagogue is someone who demands payment for giving something he has learned; the father, by contrast, demands no pay. The father is received, acknowledged, and loved. One becomes a father by grace, by discovering that one has a father, by acknowledging the gift of sonship.

FRATERNITY
OF ST. CHARLES
Passion for the glory of Christ

www.ingramcontent.com/pod-product-compliance
Lightning Source LLC
Chambersburg PA
CBHW051839040426
42447CB00006B/601